The Sufi Way
to Self-Unfoldment

Shaykh Fadhlalla Haeri was born in Karbala, Iraq, a descendant of several generations of well-known and revered spiritual leaders. Educated in Europe and America, he founded a number of companies in the Middle East and worked as a consultant in the oil industry. He travelled extensively on a spiritual quest which led to his eventual rediscovery of the pure and original Islamic heritage of his birth.

In 1980 he established the Zahra Trust, a charitable organization with centres in the USA, Britain and the Middle East, which makes traditional Islamic teachings more widely available through courses and publications, promotes the revival of traditional systems of healing and supports a variety of charitable programmes. Shaykh Fadhlalla is currently engaged in lecturing and writing books and commentaries on the Holy Qur'an and related subjects, with particular emphasis on ethics, self-development and gnosis ('*irfan*).

The Sufi Way
to Self-Unfoldment

Shaykh Fadhlalla Haeri

ELEMENT BOOKS
in association with
ZAHRA PUBLICATIONS

© Shaykh Fadhlalla Haeri 1987

First published in Great Britain in 1987 by
Element Books Ltd
Longmead, Shaftesbury, Dorset
in association with Zahra Publications

Typeset in 10½ on 13pt Palatino by
Character Graphics, Taunton

Printed in Great Britain by
Billings, Hylton Road, Worcester

Designed by Humphrey Stone

British Library Cataloguing-in-Publication Data available

Contents

Introduction

This book is based on a collection of talks which were given recently in the United States. The sixties and seventies witnessed resurgences in various spheres of mysticism, spirituality and related endeavours or topics, including the manifestation of formal prescriptive Islam in various forms. The reactions were both positive and negative, causing many people to begin to awaken to a better understanding of this ever vibrant faith, the last revealed of the world's great religions.

These talks attempt to show the gnostic and mystical origin of all religions and indeed the original creation of man himself. They endeavour to relate the inner meanings and awakenings that all these spiritual paths intend to bring about as a result of outer disciplines and practices. There can be no doubt that there is only one message in man's heart, to be fulfilled, to live a life that is honourable and fearless, that has within it no darkness, ignorance or abuse. We see, however, that throughout the ages man's history has been one of turmoil, and all civilizations, be they good or bad, have been cyclical. This phenomenon is part of the nature of creational Reality. It signifies that this existence is one of continuous change and dynamic movement. Any change implies a certain fixed parameter by means of which it can be measured; a fixed parameter that lies in man's heart and which he recognizes as being the ultimate model that is fit for this highest creational manifestation, man himself.

This noble way of living has been described by prophets, gnostics and men of awakening in different fashions, according to different cultures and times. These descriptions of the ultimate way of living show us the role man has to play in his own evolvement, by following a path of correct conduct that will lead him through dynamic action and continuous purification of intentions to freedom from useless and negative anxieties. It is as though Nature intended a certain direction for mankind, yet at the same time has given man a degree of freedom so through experimentation he may discern and understand what was originally intended of him. The sufferings and difficulties, that he experiences, act as danger signals warning him to avoid situations that will cause him anxiety and anguish. Our own inner preferences guide us to learn Nature's way.

These talks are published in their present form with the hope that they will be of benefit to other seekers of truth and those who recognize that outer material solutions, necessary though they may be as early steps, cannot in themselves bring about a state of awakening and ultimate fulfilment in man. The author sincerely hopes that the reader will find in them a connecting thread, which is man's ultimate desire for total, unconditional freedom and awakening.

PART I

Self-Unfoldment

The Model: on Body – Mind – Intellect

Who are we? If we know who we are, then we know everything. Before we can answer that, we must observe our actions, for they are the direct result of our thoughts and our thoughts are coloured by our inner make-up. In every culture, system of knowledge or religion, whatever is of any significance has its core self-knowledge. Whoever knows himself knows creation. This is the greatest dilemma which faces man, because no sooner does he try to identify some aspect of himself than he finds another and, since he cannot grasp or pin them down, he is constantly disillusioned.

So, what are we doing about this quest? In whatever we undertake we seek knowledge. Every action man takes, if we observe it deeply within ourselves, points or leads us towards self-fulfilment through knowledge. I imagine, for example, that I will be more fulfilled by speaking to people who are on a similar wavelength. Depending on the level of our intellect, mind, or upon the state we are in, we are always seeking self-fulfilment.

The body

The motivation towards self-fulfilment can be arranged in a hierarchy. The first motivation to act is physical, is that of preserving the body. Every one of us wishes to preserve our body. We need to eat and have shelter. Try to keep anybody hungry for several days, no matter who he is, and the reaction will amaze you. Nature has encoded in the chromosomes of every human being the urge to preserve the body. It is unavoidable.

What is the body? It is a complex system of interrelated physical and non-physical systems. There are, to begin with, five systems: the digestive, the circulatory, the respiratory, the reproductive and the nervous systems. Some of these are gross, like the digestive; it is earthy. We eat from the earth, whether it is first-hand, vegetable, or second-hand, meat. The nervous system is the subtlest. It is a complex network of electromagnetic grids. All these systems are interrelated with only subtle boundaries between them. Under normal conditions, when we are well and happy, there is total ecological balance between them.

The five senses of the body are hierarchically arranged from the gross to the subtle. The crudest is taste; it requires a liquid medium with which to assimilate the object. Then come touching, smelling, hearing, and lastly, seeing. These are senses with which we relate and communicate with our environment. We also have the sculptured part of the body, the hair, the skin, the mucus, the bones, the marrow. And we have something which we call the mind. There is in the Eastern system of knowledge a better description of that; it is called *nafs*, which can be translated as 'self' or 'I'. One aspect of *nafs* is mind.

The mind

We all have minds. For the purpose of establishing a basis of communication between us, we will define it as 'thought-flow'. It consists of a computer-like memory bank, which stores information from our past experience, but is activated by the dynamics of input – process – output. You only call it a mind if it flows, if it has dynamism. Otherwise, it is not a mind, it is a dead data bank. When you say, 'My mind is agitated,' that means the flow is more than you can normally cope with. 'I want to have peace of mind' means that you want to reduce the amount of thought-flow.

Because one of the characteristics of mind is 'flow', like anything else that flows it must have quality, quantity and direction. If a river is fresh from the mountains, it is pure and clear.

You will find that mind will have quality of thought, be it good or bad, charitable or selfish, constructive or destructive, positive or negative. And, like a river when it contains too much water, mind can also be flooded by too great a quantity of thoughts. Some rivers have useless direction; they may just gush straight from the mountain into the sea without serving earth or man. The thought-flow of mind may also have no direction and thus be of little use to anyone or anything. True direction is like a river which flows through an orchard nourishing the roots of the trees. The direction of thought is related to intention; the overall result is shaped according to your aim, according to the quality of your thought and the ability to maintain it.

Mind is based on the storage of past experiences. Therefore it is the seat of emotion. Many animals have a certain degree of mind. Dogs and cats, as we know, have minds of their own; that is, there are certain amounts of that quality we call 'mind' in them. But animals do not have what we call intellect, that which sheds light on the state of our mind. It is the intellect which tells us, 'All this is your emotion; you are emotionally disturbed'. How do you know if you are emotionally disturbed unless there is something within you that enlightens the mind in you? This is insight. It is like a torch, it shines to reveal what is there.

The two aspects of mind

We find that mind has two aspects or characteristics, one being prescriptive, or encyclopaedic. It is that part of the mind we use in language, science, technology, electronics, cooking, driving, etc. This part of our mind never causes us harm, as such, because we are using that faculty in a computer-like fashion; it only poses technical problems. If, for example, I am a linguistics expert and point out that you have made a terrible grammatical error, you will readily accept the correction. It will not upset you, because I am a recognized authority in that particular field. If, however, someone suddenly says 'You are ugly' or 'I hate you', your reaction is bound to be

different. It therefore stands to reason that we should aban-
don this second, psychological, or personal, aspect of mind
if we seek a rational, balanced and happy existence.

So that they do not become imprisoned by the psychological
aspect of mind, interaction between people in every worthwhile culture has been based on courtesy. In order to tackle
any system, and to create a situation conducive to happiness,
you have to have the right approach, the correct and efficient
means. The means to harmonious living in a community is
to have the correct courtesy towards the neighbours, the family, the old, the young.

We are made up of body, mind and intellect – body, the
grossest; mind, which has the characteristics of quality, quantity and direction; and the intellect, a higher, subtler attribute,
which sheds light on the condition of the mind.

Pure life and individual personality

The body, the mind, the intellect plus that subtler aspect in
us which we call 'life' result in a sentient, living person. Every
one of us recognizes 'life', for we always talk about 'my life',
'his life', and so on. Life is that element which is untouchable,
indiscernible, and undefinable. But without the presence of
this system which constitutes the 'I', it would not function
or exist. And, depending on the quality of the prism, the
light which enters it emerges with a certain colour scheme.
If it is a pure prism, it produces the full rainbow. But if the
prism is full of cracks, the colour red may dominate.

In the same way, what comes out of our prism is what is called 'personality'. Pure life, imprisoned in the body – mind –
intellect prism, emanates this so-called 'I'. If I have a limp, it
is bound to affect my personality. Or if my mind is agitated
most of the time, I shall try to hide it or put up a good
appearance. Generally speaking, I would try to hide the fault
as much as possible, because we all like perfection. Pure life
is perfection itself.

We now have a model upon which we can relfect. The

differences between individuals in this society of ours arise when we look at the output end of the diagram, the so-called 'personality'. You can say, 'I am very different from him', but what does that mean? The difference is superficial: your likes or dislikes differ. But how do we recognize this difference unless the consciousness or the understanding of liking, hating or loving is within us? The fact that we recognize, let alone condemn, someone who is violent means that we understand what violence is; its seed or consciousness is in us. When I admire someone's generosity, how do I recognize generosity unless its meaning, root or seed is also in me? When I admire someone's courage, or condemn fear and cowardice, how do I understand these characteristics unless the seed of that knowledge, the light or consciousness of it, is in me? Differences between individuals only come about when pure life has interacted through this complex being, and has emerged from it as a individual personality.

Life is one. The more it interacts with or activates prisms, the more you will find diversions and differences in the personality kaleidoscope. Therefore differences between persons are of secondary importance, because the primary cause, life, is one and the same. There is basic unity in the source of creation, there is only one Creator, and the whole of creation is interrelated because it has come from one and the same source. In essence there is no separation, but if you look at the branches of a tree, each branch appears to be different.

What does humanity mean? Why is there affinity among people? Basically it is because we have to come from the same source and have the same life essence or consciousness. Life in one person is no better than in the next.

Matching the inner and the outer

What is the root of action? Why do we do anything? We have said there is a hierarchy to satisfy our needs. All we are trying to do when we act is to create a balance, to relate or equalize the needs and expectations of the so-called 'I' with the outside world. We try to match intellectual expectations with others.

At the body level we want to relate to objects, because the body understands the physical.

The ground level is the body. If your body is unbalanced, you will find that the hierarchical priority drops to that level. You want to be well, you want to be in balance, you want to function. The hierarchy moves from the gross, to the subtle, to the subtler. That is why we say that the first thing a society needs to attain for everyone is sufficient food, clothing and shelter. These are basic needs. It is for that reason when any of us sees a society in which poverty exists alongside luxury, we know it is unbalanced and that this imbalance is bound to come to a head. Examples of these adjustments sometimes manifest themselves in full-scale revolutions or wars. The one who is hungry and deprived will come out with a gun and demand the basic requirements to preserve life. You cannot stop it. That is why we say that as long as there is poverty in this world there can be no peace. It is a hypothetical and romantic notion to expect peace and the quest for higher values as long as there are people who are hungry and have no roofs over their heads.

The mind, which is the seat of emotions and whose nature is thought-flow, tries to relate and match itself with the world of emotions. That is why you find people of similar cultures cluster together. When you say, 'We are emotionally incompatible,' it means that you are trying to match your emotional colouring and expectations with someone else's. You may say you are very compatible emotionally, but not intellectually; which is to say that emotionally, yes, you have both been spoiled as badly, but intellectually, no, she is more musical and I am not inclined that way. You must reflect upon this deeply within yourselves, and try to discover this entity, the body – mind – intellect complex, and how it tries to relate at all times to the world outside. This attempt to balance, relate and unify is the cause of all actions.

Reflect upon what happens when there is a match between you and the world outside, or a lack of it. There is the system of 'I' and there is the bigger system of the world, which is the world of objects, emotions and so on. And we are always trying to bring about harmony and unity between the two systems. Let us illustrate this with an example.

What is noise? We can define it as a form of dissipated energy which is the measure of the non-compatibility of two or more systems having interacted with or been superimposed upon each other. From the point of view of the energy level of the systems which have interacted, it is dissipated energy. In other words, the more the systems are compatibly meshed, the less noise there is. We do not like noise because we do not like inefficiency and discord. We like harmony because it is an aspect and attribute of unity.

Actions are grossified thoughts; they are the visible or tangible proof of a thought. If a thought is aborted or frustrated, then it does not come out as action. There is no clear-cut barrier between action and thought, since they are interrelated. That is why men of wisdom say your work is as good as your intention. You cannot separate intention from action. One is inward and hidden, the other is outward and visible. If we separate intentions from actions, it is only for the sake of discrimination or illustration because, in reality, where do we draw the line of separation?

Most of our actions are brought about in order to match our expectations (which are the result of pure life coming through the prism of the individual, coloured by our body – mind – intellect) with the outside world, in a certain hierarchical order and according to the energy and resources available. We tend to refine this match and continue to refine it. There is no end to the process, because there is no end to changes in us and in the world outside. The system is in dynamic flux.

At the physical level we want harmony in body, we want health and well-being. At the mind level, we do not want to be agitated. On the emotional side, we want to be loved. At the intellectual level, we want to be in environments which are comfortable to us, we want to relate to experiences based on our past habits and expectations. Our habits are based on what we have been used to.

We said that in this matching process we are trying to unify. The perfect match, balance, harmony or unity are all aspects of peace. We want peace in every aspect. Peace is noiseless, is it not? We are born wanting peace in everything. And yet we are dynamic entities; this system of body – mind – intellect is in dynamic flux, seeking harmony, peace, stillness, and, in a way, death!

The fact that every one of us wants to have a holiday is a proof of wanting peace. But we are not sufficiently driven to want a holiday every day. We hope or expect that during a holiday the outside agitations are lessened at body – mind – intellect levels and therefore we are more at peace. Even if you take a holiday to go shopping on Fifth Avenue, the motive of seeking peace is also true. You take a holiday in order to increase the possibility of the match between your desires and achievements.

Look at the average family man during his vacation. He pays more attention to his children because he is not harassed by his boss or his banker. He has more time for other things. He is less agitated in his mind. He is more charitable. If an old lady boards the bus he gives her his seat, whereas when he was commuting to his office from upstate New York he could not care less. During a holiday, there are no constant interruptions and demands and less agitation. The quantity of thought-flow is therefore less, the direction of thought improves and our man is less selfish.

Tending towards the subtle

We veer towards that which elevates us, which makes us more subtle naturally. It is ingrained in every human being to veer towards the subtler, from the body to the mind to the intellect, towards purity. We all basically want to be pure. It is for that reason we all love holidays. We all want to be on a perpetual holiday. We want to be in that holiday mood, when we are more open-minded, we have more time, more energy, less fear.

It is in our nature to be in harmony, to be in that equilibrium which we described, within the dynamic system of the so-called 'I' and the outside world. In fact, there is no separation between the two, they are part of one ecology. Separation only exists from the individual's point of view, from his expectations, his self, or his discriminating intellect.

In every aspect, we start from the gross, physical level, the body level, and then we dive deeper and deeper. These are laws whether we like it or not. All that is needed is for us to see the picture.

Action as a means to peace

We have now come to the discovery of what the motive is behind all our actions. Every action we take is in order to quiet ourselves, at the body – mind – intellect levels. Questions arise constantly in order to be neutralized by the answers. You have a question in your mind and you are therefore agitated. When both the positive and negative are there, then the agitation dies; it is neutralized. Then you are pacified and at peace. This occurs at the mental level: every action we take is to bring about peace to that system.

We are born going towards peace. Generally speaking, during the first twenty years we are children. We are growing, physically and otherwise. Usually in the second twenty years, if society, environment and culture are conducive, we try to raise a family and also earn a living, during which time we may be fortunate enough to have periods of reflection and wonderment as to what it is all about. Is it only about a spouse and children? 'Who am I? – I am born to die' is the only statement we can share at all times with all other human beings, irrespective of all other constraints or variables. The moment we are born, we are one second closer to death. A child who is one hour old is one hour closer to death, whatever his destined time may be. This fact does not change.

But is it acceptable to a normal human being that this is all? We are all born with the zest for knowledge. The first thing that a crawling child does is to explore, whether it is a pile of filth or a bed of feathers, because he is born wanting to know. But at his level it is crude; the first thing he does is to touch and put the object into his mouth. As we said earlier, taste is the grossest of the senses. The baby therefore starts at the gross and moves on to the subtler levels.

So we have discovered that we want peace. The reason we mentioned death is because it is the ultimate peace. We have come from the darkness of the womb, and return to the darkness of the tomb. And in between, those of us who have sufficient time and energy and have not been hooked by football, television or other preoccupations, can question, for our own use, 'What is the meaning of this existence?' We know it is about living well, we know it is about learning prescriptive knowledge; there is nothing wrong in this. But we want more. The more we take, the more we want; there is expansion and there is no end to expansion. The more we take of knowledge, the more we find there is, because there is no end to it. There is no end to the Creator who is the Source of all knowledge.

We said we are all veering towards peace. Peace comes to us in an instant, it is instantaneous. No sooner has what my mind set about to achieve been achieved, than the next objective is immediately set. This is because of mind's own nature; it cannot exist in a vacuum. Try to have no thoughts! We take pills because we have abused our system, and the thought-flow has exceeded the boundaries. Like a reservoir flooding over a dam we need to take drastic measures, some bulldozers in the form of drugs to plug the holes. But this is extreme and palliative. Once the mind is satisfied, it instantaneously moves towards the next desire. Once the body is satisfied with one form of pampering, it wants another. Once the intellect is satisfied in admiring this particular painting, it seeks another. It cannot stop. The ultimate peace in reality is death. But that pure energy which is in me, which has been tarnished by me, which has come from life, which has been affected by my thoughts and actions during my lifetime, that energy is not lost by death. Life is a form of energy; it does not get lost as such. There is nothing gained or lost in creation. Everything is interchangeable and is in balance. We have, for example, only recently and clumsily discovered that matter is interchangeable with energy. And we are only at the tip of the iceberg in scientific discovery of the total unitarian dynamism of the cosmos.

We are all in constant change and revolution. This is a test for you to be alert, to see, to move on, to find out that there is no end to it. Then you recognize the nature of reality. Mind is the same in all of us, although aspects of it may be different. We all have hates, loves, anxieties, fears, etc. Only the extent and outer forms of these attributes are different. Her anxieties are different from yours, your anxiety now may be different from your anxiety next week, and so on. The quality of it differs as does the quantity. Our world is one unified whole in constant flux and change, never ending, and yet simple in its meaning.

It is up to each of us to reflect upon this, to test and internalize it so that we may begin the process of awareness and awakening.

2

On Happiness

Let us now dwell upon what is conducive to peace, and what is not: in other words, what brings about happiness?

What is happiness? What is my happiness or yours? What is your happiness now, what will it be tomorrow? And when do you say 'Oh, I'm so happy now!'? Suddenly the postman comes with a letter bearing good news and you are so happy! What does it mean? If you reflect upon it, you will see that happiness occurs when whatever is desired, expected or wanted has been achieved. I desired money, the postman delivered the letter of success, and I am happy! It will probably take a few minutes before I find another thing that I want, because we are in dynamic flux and mind is self-perpetuating. The more we have our desires satisfied, the more we are happy. Is that not right? And we always want to be happy.

Again, happiness is synonymous with peace; it is matching what 'I' (the body – mind – intellect) desire with what the world can provide for me to satisfy or equalize the desire. When the match has happened, I say 'I am lucky' or 'God is merciful!' But when the neutralization has not happened, I may have doubts, agitations, discontent and unhappiness.

So how can we bring about a situation where we are most happy or least unhappy? Is it easier to be happy if we have more expectations and desires or less? The answer is obvious: less. But we are driven by our present-day culture or civilization to consume and want more.

Most of us, however, at one time or another, want the same sort of thing. At the body level, we all want to have comfortable and beautiful homes, sympathetic surroundings, fine clothes and so on. At the mental level we want to be loved, pampered, admired, and applauded. At the level of the intellect we want to be engaged in whatever is our intellectual orientation, this type of music, or that aspect of philosophy. We are herded together and there is a lot of competition, for there are limitations to goods and services available. It is for that reason that the fewer desires we have, the easier or more likely it is to achieve them. There are four and a half billion of us on this earth, and all of us want to have a three-car family and vacations. All of us want to have more and more holidays because we are created wanting peace, wanting to neutralize and match, inwardly and outwardly. We are all born to be unitarians, but we do not know it. All it takes is for us to begin to unravel what Divine Unity basically means in terms of today's culture and the so-called 'I'.

Detachment and desires

We have just found that our chances of being happy are greater if we have fewer desires. Our chances of so-called happiness are obviously greater if these desires are fulfilled. The more power we have, the more likely we are to achieve these desires, that is why we all love money. Money is naked power. Like pure, naked electricity, we can make it run a fan, a heater, a cooler, everything that brings about comfort and neutrality. It is a raw source of power with great potentialities. In every action, the subtler we become the more we veer towards purity, because essentially we are pure, for life as such is pure. Similarly we seek happiness only because happiness is our essential nature.

We are all veering willy-nilly towards the Source of creation. All it takes is for us to recognize the real cause behind our actions and thoughts. With that recognition comes real progress and awakening. If not, our way is circular and barren, constantly repeating the same pattern over and over again. But once we see what we are doing, then there is a de-clutching process that takes place. We may still do a lot of the same things, but they will not have the same influences or effects on us. There is a neutralization. We become more observant, not artificially detached.

But beware: there is no detachment as such, you are one part of the totality. Detachment is not true except in your mental attitude regarding your actions. You go up a mountain for meditation and then you hanker to know what is going on down below, and you send cables. You cannot be detached. I knew an Englishman who, after many years in the mountains of India, was left with only one attachment, chocolates. He used to walk for many hours down to a post office every Wednesday to collect his parcel of Swiss chocolate sent by friends. He was a renunciate and owned only a loin-cloth. He had given up everything but chocolate. Yet on Wednesday mornings he was like a madman.

What we are saying is that detachment is a mental attitude. It has nothing to do with what you do, or how you dress; it is your relationship with it. Ask yourself whether you are using material wealth or if material wealth is using you. Are you enslaved by it or are you using it as a slave in order to have time for what matters, self-knowledge? It is this you have to live with. You have come naked into the world, and you return naked back to the earth.

Happiness is basically an arithmetical coefficient: when you say you are happy, it means that you had a desire and that desire has been fulfilled, so the coefficient is one. You are satisfied, you are one, you are united. Now you are happy.

The more desires we have, the more difficult it will be to satisfy ourselves. If we have a hundred desires, these hundred will have to be satisfied in order for the coefficient to become one. If fifty desires are fulfilled, I am half happy. If ten desires are fulfilled, then I am only one tenth satisfied, and I compromise and rationalize. That is why the fewer desires we have, the greater is the likelihood of our being happy. Whatever desires we have – be they to do with the body, mind or intellect – they are of our own doing. Each one is naturally different, because what comes out of each of us is slightly different from every other prism. But yet, as we said, we are basically the same. The fewer desires we have, the easier it is to satisfy them. What if we have no desires?

Desires lead to expectations, which in turn arise from our actions. We all have to act, we cannot avoid it. We are questionable according to our actions, and we will benefit or suffer according to whether our actions have pure motives or expectations behind them. If we have expectations, then we are happy or unhappy according to what results from these actions.

This brings us to the meaning of pure action, acting for pure charity: the test of the pure motive is that we cannot find a definable cause for it. That is why we call it 'for God's sake', i.e. it is not for any other purpose no matter how noble or ignoble that cause may be.

We shall see later that, in reality, the state of happiness actually comes about by the removal of unhappiness. You need to act to achieve or satisfy a desire or expectation you yourself decide upon. By the removal of the potential cause of unhappiness, you revert back to the state of neutrality and happiness, Peace, peace peace... That is why we said happiness is the normal state of awakened human beings.

3

On Mind

Mind is the seat of emotion, and every person's mind has a different coloration, according to his own orientation. That orientation is what we call personality and we exaggerate its importance. We make it into a big shrine: 'This is MY personality – you cannot or must not change it!' This is idol-worship. It is worshipping something other than the real.

Mind is the centre of all these aberrations and illusions. Many of us are more emotionally inclined. Generally speaking, women tend to be more emotional because of that biological imprint to look after and serve a child, which is sometimes not a very logical process. Men, by and large, are more logical. Some of us are more inclined to action; which neither involves a great deal of logic nor emotion. It is action, and man is a warrior, a fighter. Some of us are more devotionally inclined, we want to give of ourselves. These are different aspects; we are all made up of all these basic inclinations. Sometimes, for example, one may find oneself more emotional before breakfast and more logical afterwards. The mood changes with time and according to circumstances. You must bear in mind that this model we have tried to delineate is in flux. Nothing in it is permanent. One Reality is.

Unless we freeze the world and ourselves, this situation will always be in constant dynamism and change. The ultimate freeze or peace is death. Death of what? We said earlier that we are only born to die. If you are only this physical system, this hulk, then that is that and all other attempts are futile. All that we are doing is scrubbing the body, perfuming it and ultimately preparing it for the worms to nibble upon. But is that all?

That is why we will not make progress inwardly unless the direction is clearly defined. What matters is our real inward rehabilitation. Unless there is a direction, we find ourselves meandering in the maze of what is in front of us. Time passes by very quickly, and all of a sudden we are old, ill, or swamped with the world current. We have no energy left to even reflect, let alone start the inner awakening.

The search for the permanent

The direction or goal is the news, which has come to us repeatedly through the prophets and messengers, that in reality there is nothing other than the Creator: there is only God. And everything else is a coloured, tarnished or filtered version, which can also recognize the fact that it is tarnished because there is pure life in it, and life has come from that Source which is boundless. Life continues after, but life is in me. So what is my reality? What is that which remains? What is that which is permanent (because we constantly seek permanency)? If you watch yourself in action, you will see that as well as trying to equalize, you are also trying to permanentize, i.e. you seek the permanent within you.

Those of us who are intelligent only undertake tasks which we think will have a lasting effect. We only establish relationships in the hope that they last. If you knew that your prospective employee was very brilliant but unreliable, you would not take him on. You may compromise quality and have someone reliable. Reliability means security, which implies durability, permanency, a foundation, something you can always fall back upon. All of these are attributes of Reality.

Let us examine an aspect of security. Take, for example, a good job. What does one look for in a good job? First of all, when you say 'good job', you mean that the 'job' constitutes objects (offices, people, bosses), emotions (how they treat you) and thoughts (highly qualified people). When you say 'good' that means that you have already said that the match of the world with your expectations is a good one. That is the first thing.

The next thing we say is that it is 'secure'. We generally prefer not to take temporary jobs. If you had to take one, you would say, 'Oh, it's such a wonderful place, but the work is only for six months'. This is directly related to our natural urge to permanentize and to perpetualize – to reflect or echo Reality in us. We are at our most comfortable with the familiar; we feel secure. So Reality must be the most familiar thing to us!

In a sense we are running away from some tyranny. We have discovered that in our model describing the real situation there is no inherent stability, it is dynamic. We are growing older, our needs change, and we have also logically discovered that to have a complete match between our desires and achievements is next to impossible. We are always trying, but as soon as we seem to have it, it eludes us. We discover that this matching process is at best a compromise. The balance is never perfect; yet we want fullness and permanence. We want absoluteness. It is ingrained in our chromosomes. The absolute is God.

Every system in existence seeks its cause, its roots, its origins. It is not only the salmon which struggles up the river in order to lay its eggs where it was itself once hatched. Every system, if you look at it carefully, is on its way to where it came from. If there are steel girders in the construction of a building, they start seeking their source from the moment they are erected: they start oxidizing in order to return to the earth whence the iron ore once came. Human bones and flesh begin to return to the earth from the moment we take second-hand nutrition via milk.

At times, man, that complex system, knowingly or inadvertently, seeks his cause or source, which is not known to him. As an example, analogous to the ego or personality and its cause, pure life is electric power. Electric current is the same, be it in Houston, in South India, or in Timbuktu. The nature of electricity is the same, life is the same. The way electricity comes out in its functional or in its applied form is different, i.e. the attributes are different whereas the essence is the same. There is the diffused bulb, the neon bulb, red, green and yellow bulbs, old and new bulbs. It could be an electric fan, a heater, a radio, a TV; it could even be an electric chair, another extreme. Whatever is the output, like us it can say, 'Well, I am only a green bulb!' However, it can say that it is this or that only because there is electric power flowing into it, otherwise it is a dead, useless bulb with no glow or identification. If the man is endowed with that additional X factor, life and intelligence, then he may be able to say, 'I am a man, I am Mr So-and-So, and this is my passport number, and my roles include that of businessman, friend, enemy, husband and father', and so on. But he can say all of this only because he is alive.

Afflictions

The awakening of intelligence, the first step to be taken, is this awareness. And this can only come with dissatisfaction. It does not come if we are pampered and all seems well. In these so-called advanced societies there is less and less of a real search and questioning, because everything is programmed and done for us. There are no sparks that fly and therefore no current. It is usually when there are difficulties and discontent that a person begins to ask what is the cause of his misery. Difficulties are the blessings for an energetic start on the path of awakening. Difficulty at the physical level means illness. You ask why and the doctor tells you, 'Look here, you've been abusing yourself, too many late nights, bad eating habits... It is a blessing that it is only a mild flu – it could have been pneumonia!'

At the mental level the same applies. If unknowingly you have allowed yourself to be emotionally attached and shattered, you have not constrained yourself, you have not delineated boundaries. Every system has to have a boundary, otherwise it is not a system. Every system has its outer limits, but it interacts and interrelates with systems around it.

At all times the inner mechanism is pointing us towards that which is permanent. The more we are protected, the more we have what appears to be an easy life, the more difficult it will become later on, like accumulated old bills. That is why we said that awakening of the intelligence can have a good start when the system is in disarray and turmoil. That is the best time for us to begin to reflect. Even when we are disturbed in a small way, we say, 'Leave me alone', in order to rebalance ourselves. But if we awaken more and more, then we want to have these periods of meditation, reflection, contemplation and withdrawal, so that we can look upon everything from a higher or more total point of view, and relate and integrate. Everything is interrelated, there is no isolation. Isolation occurs only when we see in small fragments. Separation only has meaning from within gatheredness.

The positive function of mind

We need to add something else to this model, which is that although the mind is the seat of emotion, it is also where we begin to discern, to differentiate and appreciate. Here we find the Eastern terminology very useful. We have to take both mind and intellect in order to show you that the boundary we have tried to draw is an artificial one, limited for use as illustration.

With proper education and rehabilitation of our mind, we bring about great awareness. In Arabic it is *dhikr*. The root of this word means to remember. What is meant by 'remember'? It means remember yourself, take stock: in other words, if you freeze the action of this complex dynamic in one photographic frame, for one second, it makes you concentrate on it, be aware of it, see it as it is. When awareness occurs in the mental zone, the intellect begins to shed its own spontaneous light onto it. This is *fikr*, to reflect or think. It is discrimination.

The higher we move, the more we become alive, aware, awakened. This is the same awareness which brings about discrimination. It is related to total rehabilitation. There is no separation. One cannot take a bit of this knowledge, or select bits of it, in order to justify whatever action or situation we are living in or demanding. If you want to have self-know-ledge, then it is about yourself, and you have only one self. We have come from the One. There is only one model, one reality. There is only one Lord. That is why it is important for us to understand and share this view of the one Reality. We move from one bit to another so that we then can see the whole integrated oneness. This is Divine Unity.

Energy and awareness

The same thing is related to energy. At a given situation or time we all have a certain amount of energy. However you like to measure it, you will find a certain total amount of energy available at any one time. Why are most of us unbalanced or dissatisfied at the moment? It is because our energy is not harnessed; we are not contained and therefore not whole-some. Part of our energy is leaking away in the form of anxiety or worry.

Self-knowledge is about wholesomeness. It is in order to see the totality inwardly, to see the absoluteness, to see the integratedness of everything, which is *tawhid*, Oneness. But, with regard to energy, if at the moment I have a third of my energy dwelling in the past, suffering from it or proud of it, and another third is concerned about the future – whether it is about the welfare of my children, my reputation, failure or success – then only a third remains. Therefore, only one third of me is really available to be drawn from now.

In any situation, the more you worry the less likely you are to achieve the expected result, because some of your energy is dissipated in anxiety. And the body is absorbing some of it in the form of perspiration, heat or nervousness. These are all forms of dissipation. So where are you now if half of you is buried in the past and the other half is anxiously concerned about the future? What is left of you?

Basically, deep down, every one of us wants to preserve and have at our control our full energies at all times. This is because essentially we all want to be aware and alert. However as we already discussed, the more we are mentally attached, the more we are concerned, the less energy we have available to us. So if there is a system of knowledge with clear direction whereby our concern is reduced, then we can say that we are benefiting from that knowledge in a manner we can build upon enduringly, not only as a brief relief like a tranquillizer or as a diversion, which does not help; for we want real joy, everlasting fun, not a fleeting pleasure.

Knowledge and awareness

This is what this knowledge means and we are all hankering after it from the moment we are born. This is the meaning of humanity. We are all the same in wanting to find that absolute truth. But if the bulb keeps telling itself, 'I am this green bulb and I have given birth to two bulbs and have this responsibility and I am contented being green and I am doing very well in this world', it has no opportunity to see that it is only a bulb because there is electricity flowing through it. Then it could contemplate the nature of electric power. But usually we do not give ourselves that chance, for we are too busy with our responsibilities. These excuses are a trick of the mind. As every system veers towards it origin, it also perpetuates or reinforces itself at the same time, whatever that system may be. If we start lying we will begin to perpetuate lying and justify it. It is our nature, it is the nature of all systems in creation to perpetuate themselves.

Every system has it own cybernetics to perpetuate itself. That is why the mind is the biggest trickster: it perpetuates what it has been used to. As we said, it is the storehouse of memory, all it knows is what has been before. We now have a new definition of our actions. Every action we take is repeating what we have liked, ensuring the avoidance of what we dislike. This is what we mean by saying it is a cybernetic or self-feeding system. Every action we perform is to perpetuate, to reproduce what we like and avoid what we dislike. And yet we call ourselves very open-minded. Where is the open-mindedness?

The objective is to be in awareness. You must simply be

aware of what you do when you are doing it, not afterwards!
There is nothing wrong in wanting to reproduce what you
like and avoid what you dislike. This is the way we are. What
matters is the spontaneous awareness of what is happening.
All human beings have the same essence and the same consciousness, because we are basically sentient through life and
life is one. The only difference between beings is the degree
of awareness.

Spontaneous awareness of our state, whether it be pleasure
or anger, peace or violence, results in neutralization of the
manifestation of these attributes. This is why we have the
ritual washing before prayer. The intention of this cleansing
is to render every moment pure and fresh, and that comes
by pure awareness. It is alertness without being two. In most
of our societies we have split ourselves, the judge and the
judged. This is because there is hypocrisy in us. Self-judge-
ment and blame are different from spontaneous, instantaneous awareness, which is the fruit of remembrance of God,
dhikr.

4

On the Self

We are building a picture of the self, the entity that we call 'I'. This self is better understood when we see that it is divided into seven different categories or levels.

The first is the grossest, the most treacherous, the most solid. It is the Commanding Self, and like a brutal tyrant, it acts entirely upon selfish motives. Neither compassion nor logic can appeal to it successfully, and it is completely motivated by its appetites and lower desires.

The next level is the Reproachful Self. It means that the hardened heart occasionally softens and a ray of conscience enters in. This self occasionally blames itself for all its usual self-centredness.

The third category is the Inspired Self. It is tolerant, creative, artistic, whimsical and vulnerable. It is an evolved self but not sufficiently for it to be secure.

The fourth level is the Certain Self which is based on certainty and trust. It is a mature and experienced self, certain that the outcome will always be good, and whenever it faces turmoil, it recalls past experiences and events to bring about steadfastness, calmness and forbearance.

The fifth level is the Contented Self and its contentment is based on knowledgeable acceptance of reality. Contentment springs from positive, intelligent acknowledgement, not from negative and helpless acceptance. It is not 'positive thinking'.

Real contentment is based on knowledge. All human beings aspire towards similar states, such as good health, good relationships, peace, etc. If, for example, ill health afflicts us, we are disturbed and discontented. On the other hand, if we are to understand the nature of the illness and the fact that it is a warning signal against worse illnesses and a chance for rest and restoration, then that illness will be accepted and the patient will be content in going through the course of the illness.

So even with an undesirable event, we can be content if we know all the factors that relate to it. The more encompassing is our knowledge of causes and effects, the more likely we are to be content with the outcome of events. For some of us, we need to neutralize discontentment and then ponder upon the total situation in order to understand the meaning. Then we may be content when that knowledge dawns upon us. The awakened being is spontaneously in a state of recognition of reality as it unfolds and thereby he is totally at peace and in contentment in all circumstances.

The next level of the self is that of recognition of total harmony, the Harmonious Self. It is the experience of harmony of the entire creation with oneself.

The previous state was being in harmony and contentment with creation. At this stage creation is in harmony and contentment with oneself.

The seventh and final level is the Fulfilled Self, complete and perfect. It is in unific equilibrium, awakened and evolved into its pure consciousness, experiencing time, yet aware and alive to its permanent divine reality. It is a self that outwardly acts as an agent of goodness and an aid towards true evolvement and fulfilment for others and inwardly is engulfed by the ocean of beingness without a beginning or end. It is the self of an outer struggle or sacrifice, and an inner contentment with infinite love.

The self is a mirror of prophetic light.

5

On Worship

We are born worshipping God. Without our even knowing it, it is in our chromosomes. In the Qur'an it says, 'We did not create *jinn* (invisible entities) or man except to worship'.

Worship does not mean that for twenty hours a day we mechanically recite prayers and invocations. It refers to what we are actually doing or striving for at all times; we are, at the moment, worshipping other objects or images. Worship means veering towards, wanting to unify with the worshipped. It is the ultimate form of love. We first like something, then we like it more, then we say we love it. A man and woman kiss. How does kissing come about? Is it not to absorb, to unify, to be one? At the physical level, we are veering towards unification. At the mental level, we are also trying to harmonize. We discovered that the most inharmonious phenomenon, which we described as noise, is when two incongruous systems attempt to unite. The more they are incongruous, the more the result is dissipated energy, which takes the form of noise.

If we observe ourselves, we find that we are always worshipping. The word 'worship', unfortunately, has come to mean something religious. Islam is not a religion – it is a way of life. It is a way of transacting with one, with everyone. It is a way of living. We are at all times worshipping, we are always at an altar – maybe the altar of helping the family, helping a neighbour, making money, painting, composing, the list is endless. We are oriented to be at an altar so long as our mind functions.

They asked Imam al-Ghazzali, the great twelfth to thirteenth century gnostic, 'What did you learn from the Sufis?'

His reply was, 'Two things. One is that time is like a sword, if you don't cut through it, it will cut you down'. This means there is no time for postponement. The matter is urgent. If we say we are postponing something, then we are only cheating ourselves, it is only a trick of the mind. Because mind has its habits now and it is difficult to see them or get rid of them, we say, 'Next year'. Next year is an illusion.

'The second thing I've learned,' he said, 'is that if you do not put yourself to work for the good, it will preoccupy you with evil'. He did not say which self, he said your self, meaning the state you are in. If you are the reproachful self, then you are constantly doing wrong and saying, 'Oh, I wasn't myself, please excuse me ...' People do not dare to ask, 'But who are you?' You keep saying, 'Please forgive me, I wasn't myself when I hit you, I got so angry'. Who are you that you are not yourself? Who are the two? If you do not make your self work for the good (good, meaning not just giving and occasional charity, but good for yourself and others at all times, by unhooking your own self-imposed tyrannies), then it is only confusion. Doing good is a displacement. We begin to change by displacement; by beginning to do a little good, we begin to crack the self and to open the crack a little more by more selfless action.

There is nothing sacrosanct about being good, except for one's own real good. If nature, if God, wanted nothing other than goodness, why did He not create it as such? Working for the good is the golden opportunity a human has to rehabilitate himself.

One does not take on goodness. The essence of goodness is already there. The seed of goodness is already in every heart.

It is like the layers of an onion. We remove one layer, and then another, and then it becomes easier. The outer layers are the hard ones. The more we unpeel the layers of the onion, i.e. the more we undress ourselves of our own superimposed layers of personality, the freer, the happier we become and the greater the chance of real fulfilment. Ultimately, when we reach a high state of inner awareness, and when we have been truly and totally immersed in that state, that inner equilibrium, we have little or no clutter left in us and that is like reaching the last, inner layer of the onion. If we now take off that layer, what is there? Space! The so-called 'I' is like an onion, it is a complex system superimposed on pure life, and life is everywhere, has been and will be. That is why we say being born is an impurity on the pure soul, like the onion being an imposition on space!

They asked the Prophet, 'What is spirit?', and he said, 'It is from the order of Allah, from pure light'. The message which we want to see and imbibe is this: you are not what you think you are. There is only God. From Him you come and to Him you return. If you see other-than-God, it is because you are looking at it through the impure prism–prison of the self. Everybody looks at life through his own goggles, and desperately tries to balance and juggle it. Your essence, your reality, is that which has no beginning and no end. It is for that reason every action you take is an echo of that reality. That is why, in our ignorance, we want to permanentize this plane of existence, because the echo of the permanent is within us. Likewise the echo of peace is in us. God is peace. All of these attributes are echoed in us. We want to exalt ourselves, because these are the attributes of the Creator which are deep in our hearts, and we have come from that same Creator.

6

On Awareness

There are primarily four clearly definable levels of consciousness. One is that of wakefulness; another level is sleep; another is that of the dream state. Every level of consciousness has its boundary and limiting factors. And when we move from one system to another there is an interphasing zone. For example, there is a brief interface between being asleep and awakening.

The fourth dimension of consciousness deals with the essential natures of life and death and their source. We all know that we will die, and this experience is entirely different from others. As far as the body is concerned, we have borrowed the minerals for a few years from the earth and then we return them by final burial. What happens thereafter we cannot describe or prove.

We know that our energy and matter are interchangeable and that the overall levels in existence are fixed. Nothing is totally destroyed, only transformed. It is therefore logical to say that the psychic energy or the electromagnetic forces which are related to life in an individual continue in one form or another after the death of the body. The imprint of the actions of the individual is patterned or engraved on this psychic energy bundle which is generally called 'soul'.

Discrimination and integration

Awareness and discrimination are the keys to intelligence, to awakening, to living fully. When you are fully aware, it means that you are living that consciousness totally. To be fully conscious in our state of awakening means being an integrated, whole and gathered being. Full and available energy is equal to being totally alive and aware. It is not, as we see practised in most religious systems, the continual inner conflict between the judge and the judged, the observation of one person by another. How can you say, 'I did a bad thing'? Are there two of you – one judging the other? If there are two, that means there is no unified centre from which you are observing. That means the inner vessel which contains you is shattered. It is for this reason we immerse ourselves in the various roles which we play in this world. But in order to switch over from role to role there is a tremendous break within us.

What do we do to bridge this gap or stop this conflict? We have to take a powerful medication: it may be drinks, drugs or any other form of sedation which does not cure. Because there is inherent conflict, there is no one centre of consciousness; because the vessel is broken, we have to patch it up. At present, the level of consciousness on which we function is in tremendous chaos. The 'I', the being, the individual, is confused, and oscillates between sets of values.

This crucial issue of awareness and discrimination is constantly referred to in the Qur'an: 'Don't you see, can't you comprehend, can't you hear?' If there is an observer and an observed, then you are in conflict. If you take the normal or practised ethics of, for example, Christianity, or the Islam of today, there are the judge and the judged. But how can there be two within the same individual? How does this dichotomy arise? It comes about because the individual is not yet awake; he is not even on the level of consciousness of being fully awake physically. He is shattered.

What should be understood is that awareness implies gatheredness, oneness, beingness and full alertness. You are whatever it is you are doing. The reason we are not totally aware is because we have allowed ourselves to wallow in all the bad habits of the past, and therefore we are wrecks, we do not know whether we are coming or going. We are walking in one particular direction, yet our face is turned towards another. Then when we trip, we say it was bad luck or the pavement was slippery. This is nonsense. They asked the Prophet, 'What is a Muslim?' He said, 'It is a person who surrenders his face to Allah'. What does this mean? The implication is that the direction of the face is the direction to which we are turning, towards our actions. If we have abandoned hankering after the fruits of action, fear of the future, and all other psychological aberrations, then that action is a pure action. This is what is called dedication to God. It is towards and for the absolute, it is for totality, and not for any specific personal purpose.

This brings us to the meaning of action and reaction. What is happening to all of us at the moment is that there is a stimulus from the outside which is received and processed by the individual, and then there is a reaction to the stimulus by the individual. At all times we are reacting and trying to lessen or relate the impact of the stimulus on the body level, mind level and intellect level; because, as we have discovered, we want at all times to be at peace. We have also discovered that the ultimate and final peace is death. The journey in life is therefore perfect from the beginning; from its inception it is a journey towards death. And what makes us alive is that power which renders this human body system sentient. But you can only truly discover this, after having seen man's systems and limitations, by taking full cognizance and awareness of it. This knowledge does not come about by analysis or concentration. If you have a task at hand, you exclude everything else and you concentrate on it. This is different from awareness. With awareness, you are simply totally alert. It is spontaneous, and as such is not directional, although it has the final resting point very clearly in front of it.

We see the quest to be in the state of awareness, alertness and beingness in those people who are more artistically inclined, such as musicians or painters. This type of self is the inspired self. It always wants to be in a state of creativity. If you take a musician, he yearns to be in the state of composing. If he is a true and great artist, he will not be composing his work with a particular audience in mind, or the number of records that it might sell. He is simply composing; he is alive. When the ballerina is really at her zenith, she is not conscious of the audience. She is alert, spontaneous, alive, she is performing in inspiration. The moment she becomes conscious of something else, she will trip. She is safe so long as she is in pure consciousness. What this means is that these types of people have that particular state of orientation over and above the usual. It is the aspect of the intellect which we call insight. The beginning of it is like a light, because light overcomes darkness. Then it becomes the inner eye of seeing. Then it becomes so overwhelming that it is only you, you are awareness personified. You are anger at the moment of anger. You are joy at the moment of joy. If you are fully aware, then you are that state of awareness at the time.

With full awareness comes full and spontaneous discrimination. It is an automatic cybernetic system of harnessing. It is not through an outside agent. Reality is pure awareness, totality, now-ness; correct conduct is the container. And the container has come about because of awareness.

With discrimination comes proper behaviour towards yourself. There is nothing sacrosanct about what you may do for your own good and what you may not do. This state comes automatically, for it is about you. You simply will not do yourself any harm and, if you do not react to yourself harmfully, you will not treat anyone else harmfully.

The beginning of awakening is simply seeing yourself as an integrated, full being. We talked about the integration of the world. The whole world is one. So how about you? You must also be one. From that centralized oneness comes full awareness and discrimination. From the one comes two. This is where the dilemma really begins. Nothing exists, be it material, thought, or otherwise, except in one of two forms or models: at the abstract level (for example, good or bad) and at the physical level (for example, hard or soft). Every mode or form has its root in the opposite. The truth is as rigid and as clear as the laws of gravity. Everything in this life is governed by laws. The reason we do not see them is because they are superimposed upon each other, and their sum total is the present reality.

We are governed by that absolute Reality which we call God. The object of being alive is to impartially take cognizance of that. If you do not see that, if you only look from an individual's coloured point of view, then there is no start. The storage area of each individual's mind is coloured differently, and therefore each person colours reality only the way he likes it. There is nothing wrong in seeing things coloured; this is also real, since every system perpetuates itself. Every system perpetuates itself because there is nothing other than perpetuity, totality, permanency in Reality. But this human entity, the body – mind – intellect, lasts only for a lifetime, and that is all. Life as such continues.

Pure action

At the moment, most of us are reacting. We have a certain concept of life, a so-called past, mind, intellectual familiarities; and we have, so far, tried to be in an environment which matches all this, so that there is the least friction. This search for peace or minimizing friction or conflict motivates us in every action. This is the matching game that we talked about. As a result of that, whatever we do is a reaction to the stimuli which come from the outside. But what is action? What is pure action? Pure action is that which we all wish to perform, or want to carry out. It is that state of the creative being – musician or ballerina – which is spontaneous and joyfully free. Why do people go through all the trouble to have a little hut without telephones somewhere by the sea and far away from everybody? So that for two hours a week Mr Smith can sit quietly and hope to be in that inspired state. What does that mean? It means he wants to be in a state where he can act purely; he want pure action. This is that state which all of us aspire to in different degrees and according to our past experiences. It is for this reason that we love the child. We say, 'Look at him, he is so spontaneous'. Why should adults not be spontaneous? Why should we not be spontaneous with the wisdom of a grown-up being, not with the child-like foolishness of a man at the age of sixty-five running around with a hockey stick? What is happening in most of our societies nowadays is that we do not grow up inwardly. We only become old and die. Pure action can only stem from pure awareness. It is up to the individual to put this reality to the test in everyday life.

The motive, as we said, of all our activities is to integrate our expectations and our state, that of the body – mind – intellect, with the real world outside. The more an individual is integrated inwardly, the more he can discriminate and appreciate the duality of forms and norms in existence. From the one comes two. From one life has come two – man and woman, and the multitude of four and a half billion of us. Your personal relationship to duality is relative. The venom of a poisonous snake may be fatal, but if we know how and when to use it correctly then it can be a tremendous blessing. The relative in turn has come from the absolute. From the point of view of the absolute, there is nothing other than pure creation. There is no good or bad from that viewpoint. That is why Allah says to the prophets, in the Qur'an, whenever they were disappointed, If I wanted to create everybody exalted in that state of being, I would have done it. But this is not what creation is about. This point appears repeatedly in the Qur'an: from the Creator's point of view, He was just created. 'Be!' And for every 'Be!' there is an opposite.

Everything we observe is in two. Everything we see is in two. Chapter 55, The Beneficent, in the Qur'an addresses the two types of Creation in detail, and there are many other references to this separation. Whatever we can see in this life, in the consciousness of awakening, is in one of two forms or norms. Much confusion arises as to why there are two, because man can only accept one. We are born in order to reach Divine Unity, in order to reach the Unity through diversity. The more the individual is unified inwardly, which is again nearness to the state of total awareness, the more he can discriminate and see duality. The more you are aware the more you begin to see the scintillating, unifying pointedness of existence. Then your actions begin to be pure. The more you are in gatheredness and unity, the more you can discriminate. The more we become alert, the more we become inwardly single-pointed, the more we observe, the more we can see.

There is dynamic interchange – you are one with the cosmos, you are the microcosm, you have everything within you. If it is not within you, how would you comprehend what is being said? It is all within you, but on a micro-scale. You are the scintillating star, you are the drop in the ocean. But there is only one drop, only one short lifetime, and if you fritter it away, you will not understand it. It is by diving within yourself that you can really understand its inherent perpetual everlasting nature, which we said is akin to, or has come from, what we call pure light; in other words, from God. You owe it to nobody but yourself, but this knowledge can only come from that inward yearning.

Outward practice as a path to awareness

Within every system of knowledge there are certain practices which must be performed. Unless the basic reasons for them are understood, these practices may appear to be only superstitious or ritualistic. We shall explore this in more detail in Part II, but let us look at some of them briefly here.

We must first bear in mind that Islam is a road towards inner freedom and abandonment. It is the abandonment of the 'I', the arrogant ego, attachments and desires. It is a system of elimination, doing without, of veering towards freedom. It is essentially based on going through certain exercises in order to make awareness habitual, spontaneous, and total. This is the reason for the prayers.

The five prayers always begin with *Allahu akbar* (God is greater). This is the highest state of the awakening of the individual, in that his first thought is that something else is greater and it is to be sought. At first we think that wealth is to be sought, because it is power which brings about a

measure of freedom. But any intelligent person able to accumulate money finds that it is not sufficiently satisfying, it
is not the greatest thing. There are still many goals and objectives
in life which are not possible to acquire with money alone.
Whatever we have attained, be it recognition, reputation or
property, we may think it to be the ultimate; but, if we are
alert, intelligent, and endowed with sufficient courage and
opportunity to indulge in the experience, a saturation point
will be reached where we find that the particular goal does
not fulfil us. We may reach a state where we find nothing
that we veered towards, nor all the objectives that we sought,
to be totally fulfilling. So we call the ultimate objective God.
That which we do not yet know is *akbar*, greater than anything
that can be perceived or conceived of. So the beginning of
the prayer is submission. You must be in tune with it from
the very start, otherwise it becomes mere superstition, without real lasting meaning. It will be a practice without a deep
base.

The meaning of fasting is not understood by most people.
Fasting is, among its many other virtues, a reminder of one's
habits. You may have a habit of constantly picking at the food
on the coffee table, as most of us nowadays do. Conscious
abstention shows us just how much we have been imprisoned
by our habits. It shows up our self – it illustrates our pseudo-
dependence on all these useless habits. Fasting calls the bluff
of the self. Like prayer, fasting is a deep shock to the entire
system. We have to use crutches in order to rehabilitate the
individual to his fullest potential. That fullness is based on
pure and simple beingness, which we call awareness. And
from that awareness comes spontaneous discrimination. That
is why we say the Sufi is a person who does not cause himself
any harm, and as a result of that he does not cause anybody
else harm.

7

On Man

The Qur'an leads us to the full responsibility of the individual, it is a constant reminder which brings spontaneous alertness and awareness. It is difficult to translate because the Arabic language is so multi-dimensional in its depth and breadth. In order to do so, it is not necessarily linguistic expertise which is called for so much as the dedication to seek out the root of every word and represent it in its total aspects. We shall now look at Chapter 76, On Man, in order to illustrate more profoundly what we have previously touched upon.

This chapter is about man – *insān*. The root of *insān* is *ins* – 'to be sociable, or on intimate terms, to be accustomed, habituated, to recognize'. The root itself is related to *uns*, 'familiarity'. We all want familiarity with other human beings and that is why we say man is gregarious. This has always been so, but it is only relatively recently that we have come to see it. Nothing is new; the knowledge has always been there. The Prophet Muhammad did not bring anything basically new. The message he imparted has been from the time of creation; the only difference was that his words and the system of knowledge were the most recent and easily followable.

This chapter contains the entire story of the beginning, the middle and the end. It is the story of humanity, of our dilemma, our search, our hankering for freedom, for happiness, for fulfilment. How to achieve it, what happens if we go off the true path, and what signs to look for, are all contained in this chapter.

> In the Name of Allah, the Universally
> Merciful, the Specifically Merciful

> Has an epoch of time passed over mankind
> when he was a thing not remembered?

> Surely, We created man from a sperm-drop,
> mingled, to test him – we made him
> hearing, seeing.

The opening of this chapter jolts us, so that suddenly it asks, 'Who are you?' Was there not a time when you were only a sperm? Was there not a time when you were not even thought of? There was a time when nobody could talk about you, or mention your name or any other attribute. This verse immediately deflates and puts into perspective your ego, fears, anxieties, lusts, angers and all other extreme moods. It appeals to the intellect, to the logic of man: 'You who have asserted your identity, your entity, you who think you are you, was there not a time when nobody could mention you? Was there not a time when you did not exist?' Then, when existence of a man begins, the start is a sperm, an insignificant low beginning. The test is to observe if this specimen turns out faithful to its simple and vulnerable start, or if it will be carried away by its self-image and arrogance. Will the being remain in 'beingness' or will he puff up his chest' and worship the images and trappings that life lures one to? This is the test!

> Certainly We have guided him on a way
> whether he is thankful or whether he
> covers up.

The basis of the mercy of Islam hinges on this verse. People talk about the way or path, but where is it? There is only Allah. He is the beginning, He is the end. This verse shows the mercy of creation; man is either going to be in gratitude – and the condition which gratitude brings about, that is, tranquility, relaxation, reflection – or man will be so inwardly agitated that whenever signs of his wrong orientation come his way so that he may surrender to the situation's reality, he covers the situation up, and runs away from facing reality by making excuses, some of which may appear logical.

What does being thankful mean? When you are thankful or in gratitude, it means you are satisfied; you no longer have a fierce hankering after something. Gratitude means a rested, peaceful and relaxed inner state; one therefore is more aware and consequently more able to discriminate – one is more fulfilled.

If man is not in a state of gratitude, then he is denying the truth, or justifying his ingratitude, his ignorance. This occurs because he has invested all these years in particular habits or expectations, a type of knowledge, and in whatever else he does. He recoils from the light of truth which questions the foundations of his 'security'. The existence of the denial of the truth is part of the mercy: because man's essence is that which has no beginning and no end, the Perpetual, therefore he wants to perpetuate his own life. To meet reality face to face is a dramatic departure from his habits.

> Truly, for those who cover up, We have
> made ready chains, iron collars, and a
> furious fire.

Although it is the present and the hereafter we are talking about, we only understand the here and now. This verse refers to the now also, but where are the 'chains, the iron collars and the furious fire'? All of us have at some point said, 'I want to be free'. We have imposed the chains upon ourselves, because of our own desires and expectations. Those who are denying or covering up the truth, who are not aware of reality who are not full, have, through ignorance, shackled themselves in chains.

The same applies to the 'iron collars'. It is the effect of an iron collar which has be to understood, that of being heavily weighed down. Look at the miserable disappointment of a person whose pet project has failed or who has been rejected by those whom he loved. It is as though he is about to dig a grave and bury himself in it. He is heavy of heart because he has identified his beingness with the project or expectation itself and therefore with the result. The result, however, has nothing to do with us; it is the by-product and we can only do our best. The more one is detached from the project, the greater are the chances for success because one has greater awareness, greater energy, clarity and thus efficiency.

Likewise we do not see a raging inferno waiting for us in the next life. We all know the meaning of fire which burns inside us when we are angry. Agitation, disturbance, anxiety, fury; these are all aspects of the 'furious fire', and sometimes even manifest themselves biologically as ulcers. This whole verse is immediate in its application. Those of us who do not wish to see reality as it is will inevitably suffer from the chains, collar and fire within.

> Truly, the rightdoers will drink from a
> cup whose mixture is camphor,
> a flowing source the slaves of Allah drink
> from, making it run in channels from place
> to place.

Camphor may not appear to us as a desirable drink, but in the time of the Prophet camphor was the main antidote available. All references in the Qur'an to camphor relate to its effect as a purifier. Those who drink camphor are those whose intake is purified and purifies – those who are therefore alive, aware, joyful and at peace within themselves. Whatever thirst they may have suffered, they are now drinking purity; they are now satisfied.

The slave of Allah is the one who wants nothing and cannot serve other than God. You cannot be in awareness unless you are enslaved by awareness. There is no freedom without slavehood, for what is the meaning of one without the other? At the moment we are enslaved by our expectations, our minds, our background, our education, our culture, this relates to the earlier reference to chains, iron collars and fire. Slavehood to God means slavehood to 'now-ness' to being-ness, to totality, absoluteness.

Everyone of us is an enslaved worshipper. If you do not enslave yourself to that from which you have come and to which you return, then you are bound to enslave yourself to other-than God.

In most commentaries on the Qur'an, this verse is referred to as the situation or condition of paradise. This however is not to deny it a place in the context of the here and now. The springs are metaphors for whatever source we desire which satisfies us, be it having a large family, wealth or peaceful austerity. Once we have completely submitted ourselves to God, we can 'channel' the springs in whichever direction satisfies us. The implication here is that the spring is within the heart. Unless the inner expansion is full, then the spring from which we drink and take fulfilment will be unavailable to us.

The inner expansion relates to the Ultimate fulfilment through inner explosion, completely surrendering and dying before physically dying. On a more practical level, it means you first have to expose yourself until such a time when there is no self, no 'I' left; until its last atom has been cracked and its roots weeded out. Then one sees life full of eternal springs easily available. And then there is no care or desire for them either.

> They fulfil their vows and fear a day
> whose evil is in flight far and wide.

This particular verse relates to the rehabilitation of the individual. It starts from the outer core and works inward towards the inner heart – we see here once again that progression from the gross to the subtle. If you do not fulfil and stand by your vows, you are clearly in conflict. If you are in conflict, then you are living in hypocrisy and you cannot even make a start. The process of bridging the gap between the promising you and the denying you drains your available energies. To be wholesome, without inner conflict, we must always do what we say we shall do. Hypocrisy is born when you say one thing and mean another. Just as energy-wasting, but more futile and childish, is saying everything you think. For every occasion there must be courtesy.

If we were alert and sensitive enough, we would im-mediately fear the result of this inner split, of this hypocrisy. This is what fearing a day 'whose evil is in flight far and wide' refers to. However proficient a liar you may be, lies always catch up with you. If you have forgotten how to live as a full being and you abuse yourself through deliberate hypocrisy, there will be a day when you will be the culmination of all your thoughts and actions. You are your own product. This verse warns us, urges us to take a good look at the consistency between what we say and what we do. It also refers directly to the day of judgement in another realm of beingness.

> And who feed with food, out of love of Him,
> the destitute, the orphan and the prisoner.

Whenever the verses came to the Prophet, there was a specific occasion. The verses are also always universally applicable, as we are exploring and seeing them. This particu-lar verse refers to a vow which Imam Ali took. He was afflicted by some trouble and had asked the Prophet's counsel. The Prophet asked him to fast for three days. From constriction comes expansion: the root of everything is in its opposite. So Imam Ali and his family fasted. Because they possessed little, his wife had baked five loaves of coarse barley bread to break the fast. At sunset, the time of fast-breaking, came a destitute who appeared at their door.

When he heard the destitute's knock at the door, Ali rose and gave him his bread; his two sons, Hasan and Hussein, also got up and in their enthusiasm gave their two loaves to the destitute. Fatima, his wife and Fudtha, their servant, did the same. They were all elated by this great act of selflessness and sacrifice.

The next day an orphan knocked at their door just as they were about to break the fast. Just as they had fed the destitute, so they fed the orphan. The third evening, a prisoner of war came to their house. He was on his way home, for in Islam no prisoner is to be kept longer than three days before judgement is passed or the prisoner is freed to return home, and this man needed provisions. The entire family gave their bread to him. That same evening Imam Ali visited the Prophet, and when Ali explained to the Prophet why he looked so weak and drawn, this verse came to the Prophet.

Look at the freedom and purity of the household of the Prophet. They do not only give what they have, but the best of all of what they have. Giving is not for the receiver but for the giver. Any good you do is for yourself; any wrong you do is also against yourself. The giving up of what we like trains us to live detachedly. When we die we become detached from everything physical, so if we cannot habituate ourselves to that now, we will not even die peacefully; we will hang on and fight it. We must give for the love of God, meaning not for the love of any other discernible reason. Then and only then is it pure giving.

> We feed you only for the Face of Allah –
> we do not want any reward from you nor
> any thanks.

There is no 'reward' nor 'thanks' because feeding for the 'Face of Allah' is pure action; there is no expectation of anything. Imam Ali and his family surely did not expect to see the destitute, orphan and prisoner again; they acted purely. Giving is a cleansing of the clutter we accumulate, not only in the material sense but also in the meaning.

One of the numerous conditions for calling a charitable act alms-giving, is that your attitude before and after the giving are the same, even in the event the receiver turns against you and shows ingratitude. If your feelings are not the same, then it is not pure action. It is not for God. If it is pure action, then you neither expect a reward nor any thanks; there is no self-interest or future investment involved.

> We fear from our Lord a day of frowning
> and fate.

At the end of your journey through life you are the sum total of all your actions and thoughts. If you have been decent, friendly, helpful and generous then you are that; you are a better being than if you had been selfish, malicious and avaricious. Next year you will be the result of your thoughts and actions now, plus your thoughts and actions of this coming year. The same applies to the point of death. This verse refers to that day as well as to the present day. If you are afraid of agony, pain, poverty or some other misery, then you will also be afraid at the point of death. The day of 'frowning and fate' is the day of reckoning, meaning that if you are afraid of adding clutter to yourself now, you will reckon and take heed now. The vicious circle continues as you try to hide the fear by inundating yourself with a barrage of mindless activities and justifications to avoid time for reflection.

> So Allah has shielded them from the evil of
> that day and shed over them a beautiful light
> and joy.

> And He has rewarded them for their steadfast patience
> with a shaded garden and silk.

To be patient is to recognize and avoid impatience, both of which exist within the realm of time. If you watch and see yourself being impatient, you immediately invite patience. Those who have 'steadfast patience' means those who shed every minute as it passes, as though they are beyond time's constraint; they are those who surrender, those who live fully. We do not know when the results of our labours will come. It is like planting a seed and then throwing it away because after three weeks nothing appeared to have sprouted. Whereas, if you know that this particular seed took six weeks to germinate, and after two years the plant would blossom into a beautiful tree, then you would have persisted longer. There is always a result for every action. Elsewhere in the Qur'an it says: 'if you do one iota of good, you will benefit from it.' You are the author of your own biography. If you have lived correctly, in awareness, fully in the now, without attachments, you will see it reflected in your happiness and joyfulness.

Reclining in it on couches, they will see in
it neither burning sun nor bitter cold.

If you are chained or wear an iron collar, then you are not
relaxed. 'Reclining' means relaxed, tranquil, satisfied. If you
are not at ease you have no ambience in which to reflect, to
begin to be aware. Nor will you feel the 'burning sun' or the
'bitter cold'. Bear in mind that the Arabs were in the desert,
where the weather fluctuated from scorching sun during the
day to intense cold at night. They will have quickly understood the meaning of that line, for always the first priority
of man is to be in comfort and physical equilibrium. The
conditions here mean that man's state is such that he is relaxed, unaffected by either heat or cold, be it inwardly or
outwardly. What is the use of having a comfortably
acclimatized room in terms of temperature and humidity, if
you are burning with anger or despair inside yourself? Man
is not held prisoner only by physical or environmental factors.
This is a description of the meaning of the garden, of what
we all want here and now.

We need to be in comfortable and conducive environments,
so that we can pay attention to the inward and bring it to
equilibrium. It is for this reason that we first want the material
satisfactions, but many of us go overboard and end up enslaved to the worship of materialism. Once one's inward state
is real and pure, then the outer situation does not matter so
much. Some people have reached such a pitch in their inner
strength that they can live on ice completely naked. This is
only an example to show you the real priorities in life.

The shade of it will be close upon them
and clusters will hang low in humility.

If you were a genius of a thief and had found some way
in which all the gold bullion in the world could be at your
door-step at the push of a button, would you stupidly press
it and have it all dumped there? There is a staggering amount
of gold in the world, so would you not have to prepare storage

for it? Would you not need vaults, banks, buildings, security and so on? In other words, you would need to reproduce the equivalent of all the existing protections where the gold is held now. What a cumbersome project! But if you could have all the gold you wanted at any time, you would not need to push the button. The knowledge that you can have it all satiates the desire.

When Alexander the Great conquered the East and reached India, he had conquered almost the entire known world. He knew of a great saint living not far from his camp and wished to bestow a favour upon this saint. He was taken up a steep, rocky path which led to a cave, the saint's dwelling. When he peeked through the entrance he saw a tiny, emaciated man sitting in the corner. He said, 'I am Alexander the Great, I have now conquered whatever can be conquered and I want to be of service to you. What can I do for you?' The old man did not reply. Again and again he repeated his offer; finally the saint said, 'Yes you can help me.' Alexander the Great was overjoyed. The man then asked, 'Could you please move away from the entrance? You are blocking the light.'

This verse refers to that condition of total satisfaction with Reality. The fruits we seek will be hanging there in front of us, within easy reach, they surrender themselves to us 'in humility'. If they were hanging in front of you, would you cut them all down and sit on top of them or store them? The verse hints that the condition of those who are in paradise is the state of contentment, of fulfilment, knowing that all needs can and will be satisfied; i.e. there are no needs!

> And vessels of silver and crystal goblets
> will be passed around them,
>
> crystal of silver they have measured
> meticulously,
>
> and in it they will be given a cup to drink
> mixed with ginger,
>
> a flowing source there named 'Salsabil'.

Here again the description of the garden and that state of fulfilment are implied. Silver was regarded as the noble, pure and
clean metal to drink from. The 'measured' amount inside the
goblet means that whatever is needed will be given, not in the
wasteful amounts with which we stuff or impress our guests.

The mention of ginger relates to its numerous good qual-
ities. It had always been well regarded as healing and soothing
by the ancient and modern civilizations in the Middle East,
India and China.

> Perpetual youths will serve them – when
> you see them, they will seem like scattered pearls.

We all want perpetuity, perpetual youth. We all want perpetual living, we all want permanency. We all seek total security, because we are basically seeking the permanent, because we seek our own source, God. It is for this reason that
when we find ourselves in a likeable situation, we want it to
last forever.

'Scattered pearls' are alike and dissimilar. When you look
at one pearl you may think it is the most beautiful pearl you
have ever seen; but as soon as you look at another, you think
that one is the most beautiful. Each is different and yet the
same. A pearl is translucent, it is opaque, it is the residue or
reaction of the living oyster. It is a result of the oyster's desire
to preserve its life, for it, too, worships the perpetual and
attempts in any way possible to prolong life. The pearls as
such emanate from a source of life. Life brings about perpetual
youth! The oyster's reaction in creating the pearl is similar to
all our attempts to encapsulate life and youth.

> When you see them then you will see
> ecstasy and a great realm.

> On them, green silk garments and brocade,
> they will be wearing silver bracelets,
> their Lord will give them a pure drink.

> Truly, this is your reward! Your efforts
> meet with thanks.

The first line refers to the seeing of wisdom and beauty in what has been referred to. The ecstasy of awareness of the reality behind all creation is vast. This is the source of all deep wonderment.

The second two verses reinforce earlier references to green silk and silver, and the pure drink, Salsabil. Silk symbolizes smoothness, lustrousness, ease and comfort.

> We have sent down the Qur'an to you,
> a sending down!

Qur'an comes from *quri'a* that which is to be read, to be recited; and what is to be read is what is already written. It means that the Qur'an is what will be. The sending down of the Qur'an is the Creation of creations. The meaning of the Qur'an is in every heart, it is imprinted in the chromosomes. It is a total picture of creation, which then came down in a verbalized form. It is what has been done, what has come from God.

> So be steadfastly patient with the judgement of
> your Lord, and do not obey any of them,
> a guilty one or one who covers up.

This verse speaks directly to the Prophet, because like all great beings who had this immense exposure to totality, to the cosmic reality, he was also human: he still had to eat and sleep. Whenever anyone exalted him he forbade them to do so. He would say, 'I am only a mortal, I will die like you'. None of the prophets accepted outward exaltation. They all had tremendous compassion for their fellow men. They wanted to guide, to help people, and when they became exasperated or impatient Allah reminded them: 'Do not obey the guilty ones.' It is a reminder that the majority of people live in the mainstream of ignorance. Which of the prophets did not have most of the people against them? This verse is a reminder to be steadfast, to have no doubts about the creational situation. It was for those people around the Prophet just as much as it is for us now.

> And invoke the Name of your Lord morning
> and night.

There are many of us who call upon God while thinking about our next meal or material concern. So what does 'to invoke' mean? If we are decent, unhypocritical, correct human beings and we invoke the name of the Creator, God (for God, is the essence – it has no attribute but encompasses all attributes), then we will be preoccupied with it. If the invocation is totally sincere and final, then the unification is bound to occur, for the bridges of separation have been broken.

This verse is talking to the coherent, unsplit, unconflicted human. From this point of view it is a prescription: if you invoke totality totally, it means you will veer towards it and converge upon it. You cannot be one hundred per cent aware unless you and your invocation become one. Your only capital is the now, and if you cannot use it now, then it is useless.

This knowledge is inner knowledge: it does not need a complex learned, mind to see it, but rather a sufficiently pure and meditative mind. This knowledge is instantaneous, it cannot be learned, one has to submerge oneself in it. That is why we say we must surrender. We can never completely surrender because we are at all times breathing; what matters is our relationship, our mental attitude, our willingness to surrender what we have specified as dear. Finally the willingness to give up the dearest of all – life, for in that lies the secret of the meaning of life itself.

> And prostrate to Him a part of the night,
> and praise in glorifying Him through the long night.

Everything has its time and place in this creation. In the daytime you care for the body: it is a launching pad for knowledge. There is light and warmth and you are physically active. At night it is easier to sit back and reflect – everything stands still, you can meditate and dive inwards. Gradually it becomes a habit, but until we consciously do so, nothing will come of it. Reflection starts with our ability to neutralize the mind. Be quiet. The ambience of the night is easier and more suited for reflection.

> Truly, these love the immediate
> and put behind them in neglect, a heavy day.

We all love the immediate, we only want now. In other words, what we hanker for and what satisfies us is immediate. It means we are short-sighted: no sooner than we say we love this moment, it disappears. Everybody wants more for putting in less. This inflationary factor is inherent in every one of us acting in this world. The cleverer we are, the higher this inflation rises because we try to put in less time and effort.

'And put behind them in neglect, a heavy day' means the more we neglect the inner health and equilibrium, the heavier the price at the end will be. We are not rehabilitating ourselves by appeasement and compromise regarding our inner state, but rather encouraging schisms in ourselves, at work, in our families and in other situations, as a result of any inner conflict.

Ask yourself what you have genuinely achieved in terms of complete fulfilment. Perhaps over the last ten years you have got a better job, a larger salary, and more worry about the high rate of interest as well as the need to protect your money or investments. Where does all this lead to? This is what this verse refers to: there is nothing left. Our lives are constantly crammed with worries, our homes are crammed with furniture, our ears are crammed with music, our hearts are constantly crammed with desires and expectations. If we stopped delaying and sat back to reflect we would begin to see what is wrong. But no, we do not give ourselves a chance. We postpone payments of bills that matter and pay up the gross material bills only.

> We created them and We strengthened their joints,
> and when We will, We can replace them with similar ones.

This refers to the same things as the first verse, which is that 'We created you from nothingness'. There was a time when you were not to be mentioned, but 'We' created you, and 'We' gave you limbs. Is it not a loss if We created you only to consume mountains of food, then only to die? But because man is the highest in creation it is for us to discover that totality from which we came. In other words, the purpose of your life is to be preoccupied with God by means of reflection upon His creation. If you are preoccupied with anything other than the Creator, you will be disappointed: the branches laden with fruit will not hang down low for this kind of life. Even if you do finally get to the other side of the rainbow, your health will not allow you to enjoy the pot of gold.

> Certainly this is a reminder, so whoever wills should take to his Lord a way.

> But you will not, unless Allah wills.
> Certainly Allah is the Knower, the Wise.

This is a tremendous verse – whoever wants Allah will find a way to Allah. Whoever wants this absolute fulfilment, this total joy, will find a way, because this is the mercy of the Creator. There is a prophetic tradition which says, 'Those who want Allah, will reach Allah.' Those who go after family and wealth will get family and wealth: everybody according to what he strives for, only if the want is genuine, if it is total, if it is true; Creation is there in order for us to be rehabilitated within it all, in this lifetime. But then again, it says that your wish will not be fulfilled unless it is Allah's wish. Everything has come from Allah, so your wish – if it is genuine and total – is with Allah's wish also, because it is ingrained in us to want the absolute, to want totality.

There are three steps – *dhikr*, *fikr* and *himmah*. *Dhikr*, as we have already said, is awareness, remembrance, invocation: *fikr* comes with *dhikr* and it is discrimination; the third, *himmah*, is energy. If there is no *himmah*, no zestful energy, then nothing happens. Every one of us has a certain amount of energy available. If it is dissipated into the yesterday, or the tomorrow, we are in a muddle. Those of us who are enthusiastic can harness greater energy: even if the enthusiasm is about

stupid things it does not matter, because later on it can be
directed into the right channel. *Dhikr, fikr* and *himmah* are
from the Creator, so they are within that law. Earlier on we
said, 'Man has been shown the way': it is either this way or
that. It is up to him. God has made this law without discrimination, an absolute law. We either take it and get on with it,
or make excuses and live in compromise and a muddle.

> He admits into His mercy whomever He wills –
> and for those who darken with injustice,
> He has prepared for them a painful punishment.

The meaning of this verse is not tyrannical, it is not how
it may appear to some. The laws – the visible, the invisible,
the physical, the otherwise – are the mercy of the Creator. If
this was not so, and suddenly, for even a minute, the law of
gravity changed, every one of us would end up upside-down
with broken jaws. It is mercy that Creation's multiple laws
govern this cosmos. It is not in chaos. If we transgress then
we suffer. Every situation is governed by law, just as every
system or organization is. Everything must have a law if it is
to function.

But what does 'We have prepared for them a painful
punishment' mean? It means if you transgress these laws,
you will be punished – you will be punishing yourself,
through your own ignorance. It says elsewhere in the Qur'an
that if you know the law and follow it accordingly, you are
being good to yourself, and if you do not, you are harming
yourself. The laws of society are made for our own protection,
but by isolating and alienating oneself from society one may
become a misfit.

The point is that we are all from the One and return unto
that One. Our failure is the separation of the 'I'. Separation
is apparent in whatever is undertaken by everybody in this
so-called advanced society. Even the language we use is the
language of war and separation – 'Wage attack against inflation!', 'Battle to fight crime!' This all implies belligerence and
division. It is not from within. The system which is totally

absolute has its own corrective mechanism from within. The system to which we subscribe even says it will annihilate itself; one or two sharp messages between two major super-powers can transform the whole world into a mass of devastation.

Man is the representative of the Creator on this earth. He is the most exalted being if he rises to that potential. The Qur'an is about that journey. The Qur'an is for those people who want to rise to their full potential, to their ultimate pure existential possibility. That is why it is a difficult book. We cannot appreciate the Qur'an unless it is looked at in context, unless it is approached with purity. It is all there for us to unravel and receive from it nourishment and guidance, in all circumstances and at every occasion.

Part II

The Gnostic Foundations of Islamic Practice

8

The Outer World and
the Self

The most difficult problem that faces any human being in this life is himself. Self-knowledge is the most difficult and the most essential of sciences for any human being. The start is the recognition that one is in this world and that one wants to know the cause of one's existence. This science, doctrine, or discipline of self-knowledge, which has been expounded by all the numerous prophets and messengers, culminating in the Prophet Muhammad, is to do with the discovery of the entity, the 'I' and its relationship to the world it finds itself in.

Self-knowledge is not so much descriptive as transmitted. It is learning by example, learning through companionship, learning from those we love and try to follow and imitate in essence and in meaning. It can only come from people who know themselves. However, the claim of self-knowledge cannot be made by anyone, for the 'I' is changing all the time and in reality it has no existence.

To understand the self, we must also understand the outer world. The outer world cannot be isolated from the 'me'. One of the first things a person learns in this world is his separateness. A child begins to observe that he is separate from his mother or parents. When a child distinguishes that there is an entity, the 'I', and that it is separate from others, he begins to 'feel' the boundary of this 'I' as being outer skin. The grosser the individual, the more you find this attitude of separate individuality and isolation. The more this happens, the more you find the individual is driven towards self-perpetuating isolation, a vicious circle. There have been, in recent times, cases of very well-known individuals who have ended up completely paranoid, afraid of their own shadow. This kind of individualism can only lead to destructive ends.

Not long ago, I was with a youth swimming in a calm sea full of fish. It was a warm day with a clear sky, and all was tranquil. The youth hit the surface of the water and could see the fish a few metres away reacting to the impact. 'The fish further away must also be able to hear and react to the impact of my hand with the surface of the water,' said the youth, 'Therefore, surely, there's a direct relationship between the movement of my hand and the fish. If they were sensitive enough, a thousand miles away the fish would hear the impact. If we had instruments to measure this event on the other side of the world, we would prove how this simple feeble act affects the whole world and, in turn, the entire cosmos, albeit minutely.'

We are not separate from the cosmos, the individual does not end at the boundary of his or her skin: one does not end here and somebody else begin there. Everything is interrelated, everything is interlocked and there is an integrated totality. Occasionally, when we take individualism to an extreme end, the system reacts from within to readjust, such as the reaction we have in the west towards preserving 'ecology'. Science too is moving more and more towards integration and overlapping between the various disciplines.

Cause and effect

So the individual finds himself in this world and he begins to observe what is around him. The first thing that is noticeable is the chain of cause and effect. An event is caused by something else, so it is the effect of that cause. If I've eaten a bad meal, I get a stomach-ache. Every cause has an effect. And every effect, in its turn, becomes the cause of yet another effect. There are no clear boundaries, only a continuous chain of reactions superimposed on other chain reactions.

What is the nature of the world? How did it come about? It didn't simply come about as a result of the decisions of the houses of parliament or presidents in the various countries.

It did not happen due to some entity called God sitting some-where and manipulating various strings and pushing buttons. How did the world which we are in at the moment come about? If we are intelligent, if we are concerned, if we are serious, if we are alive, we are bound to want the complete answer to this question.

At the moment we are considering the overall effect, the various events that have caused this current state of affairs in its total global sense. If you reflect deeply upon your per-sonal world, your current environment, which is smaller, more manageable, easier to define than the global scene, you will be able to follow it clearly in its chain of cause and effect. You will find that your world is the result of your own actions and thoughts. And there is very little separation between action and thought. You start by thought – I think I am thirsty, so I pour some water. Instantaneously, as I thought this par-ticular thought, my action began. One hand got a glass, the other reached for the jug.

Where does thought end and action begin? We cannot de-fine a boundary. Actions and thoughts are continuous. Action is the grossification of thought. Thought is the subtle cause and action is the effect. So, in my own small world, I find that I am in this particular house, in this particular environ-ment. I have this particular job, this particular wife, or these various relationships. If I contemplate further, I would find that the overall situation is the overall result of all my past thoughts and actions.

My thoughts and actions are not isolated from the thoughts and actions of others around me and the environment. Let us, for a moment, try artificially to isolate my private world, which is the result of my own creation. Why did I create my world in this way and not in that way? Let us say that this is because of my personality. Now, one personality may prefer an apartment with many small rooms. I may prefer fewer slightly larger rooms. In other words, someone else's world may be different from mine, but the cause of it, or the source of it, is not different. He tries to create, as best as he can, the world he finds agreeable and so do I. So my small world is the result of my actions and thoughts interacting and superimposed upon the actions and thoughts of the world around me.

If we dwell upon this observation and deeply contemplate it, break it up, look at it from all the different facets, we must reach the conclusion that the total global scene is the sum total or 'resultant' of all actions and thoughts combined together.

The concept of 'resultant' can be explained by looking at it from the point of view of physics. Take the simplest law, which is the law of gravity. If I move a book to the edge of the table until its centre of gravity moves beyond the edge of the table, the book will fall to the floor. There are no grey areas or uncertainties in this law. If the centre of gravity goes beyond the supportive table, the earth's pull will cause the book to fall. If there was another force, let us say an artificial wind, high velocity air blowing from under the table at the book, then you would have two forces: gravitational pull on the book, and the force of the wind upward. The book will then fall to the floor on another spot, which is the resultant of these two forces interacting with each other. In school physics, these two forces are denoted by two arrows, meeting in a third arrow denoting the outcome or resultant whose direction and length represent the combined effect of the first two arrows.

There are many physical laws in this world that we can measure and clearly define. There are also many other laws that we cannot physically or mathematically ascertain clearly. One example is the electromagnetic waves which are transmitted among ourselves when we communicate. When there is communication between two human beings, the process of cognizance is partly based on laws not yet measurable scientifically. We call it empathy to hide our ignorance about these forces.

So besides the physically definable or measurable laws, there are others which we have not yet discovered. The cow experiences gamma radiation, whereas the human being does not. Generally, animals are more sensitive to phenomena or energies which are not noticeable, measurable, or visible to us. The range of hearing of the dog is wider than ours, and so on. The intelligent observer can only conclude that there are multitudes of laws which govern this globe, and that an event takes place only as the 'resultant' of these various laws acting upon each other.

The resultant of all of these causes, the combination of all of them, results in something actually happening, i.e. the ultimate effect. There are many factors at play before anything does in effect take place.

The world, as it is, is not in my hands. It is only the resultant, the sum total, of all our combined actions and thoughts put together. So, from a scientific point of view, from an action/reaction or cause/effect point of view, it is perfection – as it is now. Nothing is missing in this world. It is all correct and everyone of us gets what he or she deserves. Now you may not like it and ask why it is like that. We ask because we are ignorant.

The world is the resultant of all of these combined actions and thoughts put together, culminating in this second, this moment, now. The next moment is determined by what we have done up to now and our actions and thoughts from now into the next moment. The extent of us taking a fresh or an independent course in the future is determined by the resultant of our new decision now and the overall effect of the past.

By way of an example, let us suppose I am floating on a river on a raft going downstream. The speed at which I am moving is determined by the speed of the current of the river, say two miles an hour. I am at the mercy of this river. This is my state now. This is the result of my past actions. So you could say that my destiny is determined, that there is nothing we can do and that man is helpless. But the future speed will be according to the speed of the current of the river, plus any additional speed I can bring into the situation, such as hooking an outboard motor onto the raft. If I can hook a ten-mile-an-hour machine to the raft, the new speed will be twelve miles an hour. The new speed is considerably different from the two miles an hour at which I was floating in the past. The future is up to us and will be determined according to the extent to which we are willing to move away from the background or past environment, or from that speed at which we are floating now. It is not a helpless situation.

The world is the sum total of all our combined actions and thoughts and the future will be determined by our combined actions and thoughts from now on. If we had the capability of building a vast enough computer model and of discerning and measuring all the various laws that govern life on earth, we would reach that conclusion. In this model, we must include every influence, including such things as sunspots, on our decision-making. Some days we find ourselves much more energetic than other days; some days we find ourselves much more generous. The weather, the effect of food in our bodies, and millions of other influences, will govern the outcome. We are at the mercy of all of these interlinked causes.

Now let us turn to the individual, to the 'I'. Every action has an equal and opposite reaction, and this world is perfect from a scientific point of view. If I abuse my neighbour one day, he will pay me back directly or otherwise. If I have abused the worker, the employer, my friends, or whatever, it is bound to come back to me. The deeper we look into that, the more we reach the absolute conclusion given to us clearly in the Qur'an, which is that if you do as much as a mustard seed of good, it will come back to you, and it is instantaneous. In reality, actions are as good as the intention behind them.

Actions and reactions, and thought and action, are not separate. They are directly interrelated. You cannot say, 'I fooled them'. You have only fooled yourself. There is nothing other than yourself. Thousands of people throughout the ages, people of self-knowledge, have reached the same conclusion. And until one reaches that conclusion, one is baffled by the world outside.

Everything has a cause. And every event that takes place will, in turn, be the cause of another event. Man and woman get together and they think that their life is not fulfilled unless they have a child. The child is the effect of this union. He, in turn, is going to be the cause of other offspring. It is a chain reaction. There is no break in all of this.

There is no clear boundary between 'I' and the neighbour in the town, and the city, and the country, and the globe. This is the beginning of knowledge.

Duality

As we said before, when the observer begins to go deeper into himself, and into his surroundings, he finds most phenomena exist in duality. We begin to see twos. If we look in the middle, it may be confusing, but if we look at the whole spectrum we see twos clearly. We see black and white. If we look in the middle, we see greys. If you go to the extremes of anything, you will always find two aspects: day and night, illness and health, peace and war, good and bad, etc. Look at the extreme poles and see the shades in between. Often there is no clear-cut boundary.

Look at life and death. The flower that is wilting, that begins to smell bad, that begins to decay, heralds the beginning of a new flower because it will be compost or fertilizer for the next one. Man begins his life journeying towards death. The minute he is born, he is closer to the end of his journey, closer to his death. Yet man nowadays avoids the question of death.

The most logical subjective statement man can make is that he is dying. It is a universal statement. And yet nobody wants to know what the meaning of death is. What is the end of this journey to death? Is that the end of the story? When you tell me that my work location is transferred to a new town, before you finish the sentence, I ask you for a map of the town. What does it look like? What is the population? What is the weather? We don't want jolts in this life. We want harmony. Jolts dissipate energy and we want to preserve energy. And yet, death is the most certain thing and we do not ask the meaning of it.

What happens when we die, and what is the experience of death? The Sufis say, 'Die before you die.' Here they refer to the *death of meaning*. This death implies being absolutely still, implies having no thought in your mind. Every attempt we make in this world is to reduce the quality of thoughts in our mind. Catch yourself at whatever you are doing and you will find that you are doing it in the expectation that your mind will become quietened by it.

We see duality in whatever we are witnessing or effecting. If I am well now, I can only be ill next. There cannot be any other choice. Existence in this world fluctuates between illness and well-being. If I say I am happy now, I am in a good mood, the only thing that can happen is to reach a bad mood, because everything is in dynamism – life and death, black and white, up and down, day and night. They revolve. Each one extreme contains the seed or secret of the other. Day causes night and night causes day. Every one of these extremes has its root or sources in the other extreme.

In order to see extremities clearly, the best place to be is at the centre of the spectrum. If you are at one extreme, you *are* the extreme. Our senses have limitations. My hearing range stretches only between certain wavelengths. My vision, according to the strength of my eyesight, has a range. If I place myself in the middle of the range, then I can cover the entire range. Take love – hate. If I am at the extreme of love, I am missing the entire range, because the other end of it is hate. If I am in the middle, if I am balanced, then I can cover a greater range of experience, and therefore knowledge. This is why moderation in every state is advocated.

The material world

When man begins to question what he sees around him, he observes, then reflects, then goes deeper into contemplation, which is also more disciplined, and then into more profound meditation. To meditate means cutting out anything other than what is being meditated upon. Usually, we are exercising our discernible faculties, our intellect, our mind, our quantitative faculties, measuring all the time. Am I getting the right deal? Quantitatively, most of the time, qualitatively sometimes. That is why we are so rich outwardly in this world and so poor inwardly. We have accumulated the greatest riches in terms of material well-being. Everyone of us is cluttered with belongings, houses, cars, boats, relationships, and whatever. Yet, in terms of real quality, we are poor. That is why we have the television or radio on all the time, to fill the empty space. This is the state of affairs we are in, and we are not only a description of the reality, but we *are* this reality.

The world of matter does exist. The human being, the 'I', is made of matter, minerals from the earth, in order to enquire and understand the cause of his beingness. There is nothing wrong with matter. We have not created matter. We do not even know what it is. The more we explore the nature of the sub-atomic world, the more we discover we do not know, and that the final, fixed, basic building-block of matter is elusive and vague. We now find matter and anti-matter in dynamic flux in the world of physics.

Fragmentations of the self

What is surprising is that we talk about 'I' very flippantly, as though it were a concrete thing. It is very seldom that we stop and reflect upon who the speaker is. The reason that we often do not reflect is that in the particular context in which we say 'I' there is an image or role behind it. It is usually a definable image – the father, the friend, the leader, etc. – an image that you have built around yourself and which has somehow taken on a shape. What is this illusive 'I' which finds itself in this world with which we tried to establish a relationship?

There are usually multitides of 'I'. There is 'I' the family man, there is 'I' the angry man, the good man, the traveller, the businessman, the father, etc. There is the 'I' who is secure, happy, concerned, irresponsible, guilty, ill, etc. These are all fragments, and this fragmentation is the result of our inner fragmentation.

In order to cement the pieces we need constant assurance from outside agencies, such as the people around us, society at large, the media, etc. All of this is to prop up the fragmented being and make him feel he is whole.

The Path

We will not understand the world unless we understand the individual. We will not make headway unless we understand the self, which manifests as the 'I'. Thus, we want to reach the cause of 'me', this 'I'. All of us, one way or another, are trying to reach that point. Unless that attempt is a disciplined one, unless it has its doctrine, unless it has its own boundaries, it is a haphazard journey. As with any other area of study, we need to have the methodology clear, the hypothesis defined, other tools at hand and some idea as to the ultimate end we seek.

The difficulty arises when we have identified with the gross world and are living in distracting environments, when we have become so materialistic and neglect everything else. It is difficult to pursue self-knowledge outside a fairly defined discernible arena. And this is the meaning of the Path. Path implies constraints. A path is contained between boundaries and has disciplines. Every path has its codes of conduct. We cannot just meander around on a path because there are others on the path. Path takes us from one point to another. It is made to ease a journey – from the point of ignorance to the point of knowledge, from the point of misery to the point of inner happiness and self-fulfilment. The science of self-knowledge is about that. And if the path does not lead to that, it is not the true course. It is meaningless, another dogma. Basically, there is a discipline, needed because the chances of reaching that ultimate point of certitude and knowledge are very slim.

As we said in Part I, we have a body and a mind, the seat of emotion, and we have the intellect. The more we allow the intellect to develop, the more we know what is basically right or wrong, and the more we see the common denominator for basic behaviour of people.

What we are doing in this world, every one of us, in every instant, is trying to balance the individual world, body, mind, and intellect, this so-called 'I' with the larger world of objects, emotions, and thoughts.

The ultimate objective of our quest in this life, while alive, while functioning, with a sane mind is not to have the memory of the past and the expectation of the future filling us to the brim. In other words, to get rid of the 'I'. The man on the raft in the river may be intellectually aware, but yet he has not done anything to change his condition in reality, inwardly.

Self-knowledge is the science of inward freedom with outward constraints. Inwardly joyful, outwardly sober. Man is the seeker of this course. This is what motivates us.

9

Self-Fulfilment

As we have said, the individual responds to stimuli which come from outside and reacts according to his memory bank, and every action we undertake is the grossificiation of a mental demand or process. All the time we are trying to repeat a pattern that we were familiar with in the past, to avoid pain and to invite what we liked. We are trying to quieten the mind all the time.

If we are fairly healthy, if our emotions are not paining us, then by and large we can see a common denominator, which is an intellectual activity. If we do not have an emotional bias and we are travelling on a road with a knapsack full of food and we find three hungry people on the wayside, something is bound to stir in us to tell us to share. The more we get closer to the source of consciousness, the more we find that humanity has a common source. Correspondingly, the more I have identified with my various roles with my emotional and mental attachments and expectations, the less fulfilled I will be.

As we said earlier, happiness is a coefficient, which equals the number of desires achieved over the number of desires one has. We discovered that if one has no desires, one can, at all times, have a coefficient of 'one' for happiness – the only state of permanent contentment. The answer, as we have seen, is to have no desires.

Now, how can you have no desires and be active in this world? And what are the causes of these desires? What is the mechanism that causes all the insecurity and anxieties that we have in us at the moment?

What is anger, for example? If you catch people in the state of rage or anger, or better than that, catch yourself while you are angry, you will see that this is the extreme form of exhibiting your reaction to desires unfulfilled. Take a simple example. The child has discovered that chocolate gives him pleasure, and his mind is relatively quiet while the chocolate is melting in his mouth. Then he wants to go for it again, but the mother thinks it's not good for him and he is deflected. Therefore he cries.

The adult does the same thing. All that happens is that because of society, because we have to live close to others, the adult curbs his anger. He is angry because he did not get what he wanted, but that anger is curbed in him, which could result in other problems, such as ulcers. You cannot separate the mind from the body, from the intellect. They are interrelated.

Seeking the cause

Once we have satisfied our body, we are well, once we don't have urgent emotional attachments or concerns or worries, then we veer more towards the subtler activities and the so-called cultural activities. And this is a process of broadening, a process of expansion. You will find also in worldly activities, the higher the sight of the individual is, the greater are his achievements. In other words, if the world of the individual is only himself and his family, then it is a small, limited world. And, if he takes on a whole community or a country, then his world is much larger.

We have ingrained in us this search for knowledge towards the higher, towards the subtler. As we have said, once the gross requirements are satisfied in us, we go towards the subtler. Once we recognize this, then the process becomes swift. Man's position in this world is that he is a seeker of his cause. The division between spirituality and materialism is artificial. Man functions through this instrument, this complex body, and there is no separation between it and his 'spirit'. Because we are not satisfied spiritually, or internally, because we have not got inner tranquillity, we try to satisfy more and more externally. And that is why we have ended up swamped by quantity at the expense of quality: more and more objects and things, and less and less profundity and quality.

Our basic heritage is tranquillity and peace and completeness. We all veer towards the same course, towards God. We all are functioning because of life in us. Life comes from God, the Creator. So, in every action, trying to satisfy our desires, we are actually on the path towards the Creator. The only difference is that most of us do not recognize it.

We all want happiness and we define happiness as desires achieved. When all desires are achieved, we say, 'I am tranquil.' Well, why can't we be tranquil to begin with? Who made me have all these multitudinous desires? There are basic needs, but we don't suffer from the lack of those basic things now, things such as shelter, clothes, food. It is ingrained in us, in our chromosomes, to keep the body alive as well as we can, in order to discover the purpose of it all – that is the purpose of living.

Man is the seeker of his cause. The closer he gets to it, the more he realizes that the basis of happiness is self-fulfilment. It is I who decided that unless these desires are satisfied I am not fulfilled: a job, a good position, a good salary, a house. The man on the island off Malaysia has not got the same desires, he has others. Yet it is the same process. It is the individual who decides. And when on occasions he is fulfilled, he is at a point of tranquillity. We all want tranquillity. We all want peace. But if we do not have peace from within ourselves, we cannot have peace outside.

Nothing and no one brings us happiness; it is the removal of unhappiness that takes place. I am poor. Now I inherit a fortune, and what happens? Poverty is removed. Money did not bring me happiness, it removed unhappiness. My unhappiness is different from anyone else's. If I do not want belongings, then I suffer from having an excess of belongings, which is another way, more subtle and more difficult. 'I don't want anything. I'm going up to the mountain and I'm leaving all this behind!' But you cannot run away from the world. You

cannot run away from yourself. It all hinges on our relationship with the world, our mental attitude towards the world,
our mental attachment to the world. There is nothing wrong
with worldly objects as such.

Surrendering attachment

Nothing is wrong with the world. There is nothing wrong
with creation. Everything is in a perfect form in its perfect
place at the perfect time. It is my attitude towards it which
causes me pain. The postman arrives and there is a letter for
me informing me that a house in the countryside, which I
love, has burned down and the roof has caved in. Those
wonderful antique paintings are completely ruined. I am in
ruins!

The Sufi (gnostic) says you have to surrender. There is
nothing wrong with the house provided that when it col-
lapses, you do not collapse with it. It is the surrendering of
the ownership/attachment aspect of it. The fact is, you can
only carry out an activity efficiently if you are not attached
to it. You can only run a business efficiently if you are not
attached to it.

The seeds of all emotional attributes are in us inwardly,
otherwise we could not comprehend them when we see them
outwardly. The seed of fear is in us, thus we all know what
fear is. We all understand what pain is. We all understand
what anger is. We understand all these things because we
are all from the same source. We are all creatures of God, we
have come from God and to God we return. We have all been
created in the same manner with the same consciousness.
We are all the sons and daughters of Adam. And, therefore,
from that point of view, 'I' the individual, the microcosm,
reflect and contain the characteristics of the macrocosm. This
is my little world and that is the entire world. But in my little
world are to be found the miniatures of the outside world,
and, therefore, the secrets of the outside world. We say we
are looking for self-fulfilment. So there is nothing other than

your own self-fulfilment. And that can only come when your mind is quiet.

Inner peace and correct conduct

Quietening the mind is achieved only by discipline and proper behaviour, by living according to proper laws that govern all interactions. This is what is called *sharī'ah*. So far, what we have been talking about is *haqīqah*, the inner reality: the individual and the secret of beingness and unity. In order to contain and conserve energy, the individual must move within certain boundaries, be governed by certain basic laws. The source of this knowledge is imprinted in the chromosomes of the individual. 'Don't do to others what you don't want done to yourself.' This is the basic of all moral conduct – the basis of all religions before they became tarnished and adapted, and all sorts of superimpositions were put onto them. It is the absolute code of behaviour. Unless we have correct outward behaviour, we cannot change inwardly.

The 'individual' is the product of all past actions and thoughts put together. If I am tidy in mind and healthy in body, you will invariably find the place in which I live also tidy and the food that I eat wholesome food. You could not be eating bad quality food and maintain a healthy body. Ultimately, you are what you eat. If I maintain a proper diet and live in a healthy manner, not overdoing it, in balance, then I have a balanced body. So, from the physical point of view, I am the product of what I do. See where a person lives and what he eats and you will know what he is. The outer and the inner are related. You cannot be tidy inwardly and confused outwardly. Invariably, the vessel oozes what is in it. You can hide it occasionally, just before the guests come you tidy up the room, but, as soon as you relax, your reality will show up. If you are a violent man, if you are a sick person, you can only be what you are in the long run and show it outwardly.

How can we begin to behave in a manner that is going to make us more self-fulfilled or happier? We are in this moment, in our normal state of behaviour, acting according to outside stimuli. All of a sudden I see something happening – I match what is happening with the likes and dislikes in my mind and intellect, and I react towards it. Stimulus – individual – reaction. This is really our norm. Somebody says something that is nasty. I react and say, 'Don't be rude!' Somebody says something that I like, I react to it and say, 'You are right.' All the time we are taking in what comes from outside and reacting to it. Like reaction boxes.

How can we, as individuals, act rather than react? Take this simple checklist and discover for yourself. If the answers to the questions are no, then you are acting. Otherwise, you are reacting. Am I doing this in order to repel fear? To increase my security? Or my image? Or my position? Or my wealth? Through vanity? Anger? Fear? Love? Hate?

If my response is spontaneous, for God, not for anything else, then it is pure action. Only then is it spontaneous and correct action. Otherwise, it is only reaction. Every reaction leaves its tarnish on man. Every reaction accumulates additional clutter in man's mind. The subtler the tarnish is, the more difficult it is to wipe it off. This is the problem with all religions.

Islam is a way of living. It is a life transaction, and not a religion as such. Our blessed Prophet lived as a man, and we know how he lived. He traded, travelled, lived with his family, laughed, played with children, a smile always lit up his face, and he was generous. He was self-fulfilled. The self-fulfilled man lives every second of his life fully, to the brim.

Unless man is acting, he is reacting, because life is not a vacuum. The mind cannot be neutral or empty. You are either full or not. Life is dynamic. From the moment we are born, we are hooked into this dynamism until we die. We are enslaved by this reality. We are enslaved by God. And the purpose of existence is to recognize that the cause of what makes us happy or miserable is in our hands.

You find everybody encourages generosity. This is only in

order not to have attachment to wealth. It does not mean that you take a suitcase of dollars up a tower and throw it down. What is prescribed is lack of attachment to an image, a reputation, a physical entity, a mother, a father, or anything. Again, lack of attachment does not mean disrespect. If I am not attached to something, it does not mean that I go around kicking it, saying that it does not exist. I use the object when it is available to me and do not worry about it when it is not. When the need arises, we try to obtain the required object, but if we do not succeed, if this door is closed, we try other doors. We can only walk through one door at any given moment. We can only take one breath at a time. We can only hear one word at a time.

So we are beginning to come closer to how we as individuals can conduct ourselves in this life in such a way that from both outside and inside we begin to be contained. We will find many things to help us to relinquish ourselves and bring us nearer to submission to the Real. By cutting out all the self-inflicted clutter, we eliminate the non-real and the Real will be there. By eliminating what is self-imposed, the true self is illumined.

In order for us to have inner discipline, in order for us to begin to gather ourselves together, to control the mind, to hook onto the ultimate, to begin to live fully, to have fewer problems and desires, each one of us needs slightly different orientations. We need constant reminders in one form or another. If I am agitated and I say, 'Thanks be to God', I am bound to deflate that which was causing the trouble. If I do not sing the glory of God, I would be singing the glory of other-than-God – this thing, that fellow, or my wife, or mother, or country, or whatever. We adhere to outer discipline in order to bring about inner cohesion and discipline. The non-separateness of man from his world, the non-division between outer and inner, is that there is nothing other than God.

10

The Path of Self-Unfoldment

What is it that screens us from reality or prevents us from living self-fulfilled and by God? The Arabic word for it is *wahm*. *Wahm* is illusion. It is like the film of the past in the mind. It is illusion which envelops or screens reality. It is illusion that is the barrier. So, if illusion is removed, then vision or witnessing must take place. It is because of illusion that we do not know God. But whoever has remembrance and discrimination and yearning is the man who will absent himself from illusion by insight. When you make yourself absent from illusion, clarity begins to take its place.

The freedom we are seeking, the objective of beingness that we aspire to, can be achieved if we act and do not react. We have found that the pre-qualification for that is to be empty, to be clean, to be clear. It is not to have standards of mental expectation to which we relate what comes to us from outside and then match it and simply respond in an automatic manner to it. This is not easy, and yet it is easy. It is easy because it is our real nature to be spontaneous, to be alive, to be inwardly free. We are all seeking these attributes. We are all aspiring towards inner freedom. The habits of twenty, thirty, or forty years, whatever our age, cannot be wiped away in one, two or three days. Even a machine that has been used to a certain tempo of existence cannot be retuned to an entirely different phase immediately. It will seize up or generate other problems. So time is necessary and patience is necessary. But time is also treacherous, we must act both urgently and patiently.

The most important requirement is energy. By energy, I mean the extent of yearning. It is the energy that makes us desperate for that state of beingness that we are talking about, which is the state of total inner balance, tranquillity, peace, submission. It is the fuel that sends the rocket through the barriers of the self. No matter how much intellectual understanding we have of the science of self-knowledge, it is of no use and to no avail unless we are desperately, earnestly, honestly striving towards God. The extent of this yearning is related to the extent of non-hypocrisy in us.

The Qur'an attacks hypocrisy. The hypocrite is someone who says something which he does not contain or mean inwardly. In other words, his tongue is separated from his heart. His mind is separated from his heart, or from his innermost core. There is, therefore, a conflict, a break or separation in his inner being. This conflict is the same as the separateness of the 'I' from the world. If I say something to you with my tongue that is not backed by my heart, I have created a separateness of the 'I' from the world. If I say something to you with my tongue that is not backed by my heart, I have created a separateness in me, an inner conflict in me. So the sufferer is 'I'.

The basis of honesty, the basis of decent behaviour as we all know and accept, is to do what you say you will do, to keep your contract. In other words, connect action, which is the extension of your thoughts, and thoughts, as expressed by your tongue. But we often say things which we do not mean. And the immediate result is lack of respect for me by me. When a child is crying and I want to quieten him, I make a promise which is not meant. By trying to fool the child, I have fooled myself and lost the child's trust. So you must do what you say. Until recent times, people in business used to say, 'My word is my bond.' No longer. There is no bond any more. Most bonds are broken.

The second condition of honesty is a higher level of self-respect, of beingness, and that is, you must say what you mean. In other words, there is no gulf or separation between your tongue and your heart. If I say I like the colour of this jacket, I must mean it. Thereby I am whole. If I am trying to please you because I need your assistance or power, and I say how nice it is without meaning it, I have created a break or conflict within me. There is no honesty in this, no truthfulness.

The third thing about truthfulness, which is subtler and more difficult, and is the beginning of wisdom, is that you do not say everything that you think. Supposing I do not like this jacket? There is no point in my saying so. No positive purpose is served by my saying it. It is a waste of energy and time. So preserve the energy. But we have fogotten how to preserve the energy. Our energies are all dissipated because we are fragmented, like broken dishes, shattered, and not able to contain anything.

This basic human behaviour is what we call *adab*. *Adab* is the science of correct behaviour and interaction in different situations. Every situation has its *adab*, its code of conduct and behaviour. When we are playing with a child, there is a certain correct behaviour. If you are transacting a business, it has its code of conduct. You do not, all of a sudden, pull the man's arm and place him on your lap, as you might do if you were playing with your child. When you are learning something which is subtle and profound, there is a certain way of doing it. If you do not have the right approach with God, you will not arrive.

Correct conduct is what causes the proper interaction between the doer and the situation. Therefore, it is the connector, the unifier. There is nothing other than unity. There is no separation. Separation is our own illusion, created by each individual especially to envelop himself. What is the way out of this? How can I, the individual, the sum total of my past actions and thoughts, superimposed by the actions and thoughts of others, see this? The situation now is not a result of chaos, because for a thing to have happened various laws, physical and non-physical, must have taken place on this globe.

When the Prophet was told that something undesirable or wrong had happened, his answer was that, because it had happened, it must have been meant to happen. This is not fatalistic. It is perfection. It means that if we could really measure all the various forces at play, then we could see clearly and understand why the event took place. Because I was in a hurry and there was a banana skin and I did not see it, I slipped and broke a bone. The whole thing is due to my ignorance, my lack of knowledge about the banana and the situation. So I was careless and the price for it is this disaster. There is nothing to it. It is not to be judged, or given a moral value, for the penalty is inherent in it and is automatic. There is no guilt in it, but our society is guilt-ridden. That is why we must constantly, outwardly and inwardly, integrate ourselves by constant reminder to cut out the past.

In Islam, we wash in a prescribed manner before prayers, which is an act of cleansing, both outer and inner. If you concentrate on it, you are cleansing in a total manner. And if you ask forgiveness, and it is meant – if you really mean it – then you are forgiven, and the tail of the past is cut off. If you really mean you are sorry, you do not even have to say it – the result will be there. What matters is the heart's intention. When we mean it and say it, we integrate the outer and the inner. Otherwise, it is ritual. Ritual alone is of no value. It is like a shell, like a container. What is the use of a container if there is nothing in it? But nothing can be contained unless there is a sound container.

Integrating the inner and the outer

So we have come to the question of how do we integrate inwardly through the Path. In the Qur'an it says, 'and whoever wants to reach will find a way to God'. Those who are serious in the quest, those who are desperate, will find a way, because the way is from within you. The way is not from outside. Now, because of the complexity of the outer situation in this world, we desperately need to follow a clear-cut way outwardly, before we can recollect inwardly. So we depend on *sharī'ah* (code of conduct) and *sunna*. *Sunna* is the way the Prophet behaved and acted. This is well documented and authenticated; we have many independent sources which confirm what he said and did.

If we start properly following the Path, we soon reach the conclusion that the proper code of conduct, the only code of behaviour, is actually known to all of us from within, if we reach down to the base of it. But we don't often do that because we have many barriers due to our own mental images, expectations, and habits. Those who are on a strong path towards God often break habits in order to soften the mind and free it of past images. So you become creative, and your energies are available and expand you to wider fields, not in a haphazard, grasshopper-like manner, but in an inspired manner. You are available, you are living now. You are not half in the past and half worried about the future. If that is the case, where are you now? This is the way most of us go through life. And then we blame it on luck or circumstances. It has nothing whatsoever to do with anyone outside you. But it is always easier to blame others and thereby protect the self.

The Prophet lived fully. He fought when attacked, he transacted business, he loved those around him, he kept a straight path, and lived a simple, pure, joyous life. He lived the entire spectrum of humanity. It is the same with the other prophets, if we arrive at the true characteristics of their behaviour.

Dhikr, fikr and himmah: remembrance, discrimination and yearning

The Path lies in *dhikr*, *fikr* and *himmah*. *Dhikr* is the remembrance of God, from whom I am separated by my self. It is this illusion that is caused by me that is the cause of this barrier, separation. So it is a process of elimination. If I overcome the self, if I remove all of these images, all of these goggles that I have erroneously put on, then I am bound to be less separated from that which is the source of all beingness.

So remembrance is necessary for us to begin to dissolve the self. If I remember God at the moment of agitation and disappointment, if I remember the Creator of the entire cosmos, from Whom this life is allotted for a few years, then my own little misery, my own problem, put in the larger perspective, is bound to gain a measure of relief. It is bound to be a remedy for whatever situation I am in.

Remembrance begins as an outside activity. Then it belongs to the heart. How can I remember God when I am full of me? When the bucket is full of me, there is no room for anything else. It is a displacement process. A bucket of pure water with mud particles in suspension can be purified again if we place it under a tap which drips into it fresh clear water. In time, this bucket of mud begins to get clearer and clearer and begins to reflect more of its real nature of pure water. Our nature is that of purity. That is why we like purity – we are basically pure at source. So there is no room for personal guilt. Our heritage is purity and the simplicity of beingness. But, because of the activities which we undertake in the world, we begin to solidify the roles and images into a personality with apparently conflicting and often irreconcilable aspects.

It is by remembrance of God that I can begin to melt down the layers that I have created which are the source of my agitation, problems, and expectations. It is the most vital activity. A muslim prays five times a day, five formal and definable times for *dhikr* and *ṣalāt* (prayer). Five times to remember and submit to Allah, outwardly and inwardly.

Fikr is that light which is shed on a scene in order to discriminate: what is good and what is bad, what is lasting and what is not, right and wrong, black and white. If we are in a state of real remembrance, then discrimination will operate spontaneously.

Suppose we stop the moving film of our actions and freeze a frame. *Dhikr* freezes the 'frame' of action and *fikr* shines the torch of discrimination on it. Subsequent correct action will result fom this. The film shows that I disliked your presence here to such an extent that I proceeded to punch you, and all of a sudden I see myself in this childish act, in the frozen shot of this film. If I catch myself in that instant, I am bound to discriminate and immediately correct the course. But we are often slow, and leave it too late. After I have done it I plead for forgiveness and say, 'It wasn't me!' What this means is that, after the event, I have had a replay of the act, because it was fresh in my memory, and in the light of discrimination.

Neither remembrance nor discrimination will occur unless there is *himmah* – energy, yearning to be true, full, alive. The more we have this energy, the more it becomes available. It is like tapping a source: the more you clean the head of the spring, the more clear water will flow. But because we are accustomed to living in a manner that is totally incorrect and harmful, and which we try to preserve, we are scared of change and shut ourselves up in our private rooms. It is because we want to preserve habits. We are afraid of opening our hands to drop the thorns which we have clasped and made ours. But, when the pain is deep and real, then great yearning will enable us to act, drop the thorns and find the freedom that was there to begin with anyway. You may ask, 'If it is so easy, then what are all these methods for?' In a way, it is like picking up new thorns at will in order to get rid of the thorn that has been aching in you all these years – the old self.

So there must be a beginning. The extent of the new speed of the raft, floating on the stream of the past, depends entirely on the extent of the new energy in you. The greater the yearning and the burning, the greater the energy. The greater is your suffering, the more you are qualified to free yourself from it. When fear is mild, one can brush it aside. When it is vast, new basic treatment is necessary and final cure is more probable.

So the three basic requirements of the Path are entirely interrelated. Each of them reinforces the others, both in quantity and quality. If I have greater awareness, then more discrimination will constantly illuminate my actions. Therefore, more of my new actions will be such that they are not likely to enhance the self in me. Slowly, one observes the vanishing 'I'-ness: arrogance, vanity, personality. So the outcome of the path towards self-knowledge is getting rid of the impermanent. Get rid of the 'I' and you will see the real self. It is a process of elimination. The embryonic seed of real knowledge is in everyone. But, in most cases, it has been tarnished or covered by the layers of the personality.

> And those of you
> Allah has been most generous to
> are those who have the greatest *taqwā*

Taqwā is fear of God, devoutness, submission, and piety. Orientate and tune towards it. There is nothing other-than-God. There is only God.

The Qur'an says that Allah is closer to you than the jugular vein. What could be closer to you than that? There is nothing other than the oneness of reality, from which we have all of these attributes, phenomena and characteristics. There is nothing other than that oneness towards which, knowingly or not, we are veering. In most cases we veer in a zigzag manner. Because we have collected so many bad habits, we need to emulate, to copy, and to have a living example to follow. That is the Path's provision.

The science of the self is learned by transmission and not by prescription. It can be gained by keeping company and by example. Children follow the example of their parents. That is why parents are often ashamed when their child is misbehaving. The child is actually betraying the parents' reality. He is a mirror, a reflection. He has seen them quarrelling all the time, therefore he quarrels.

Wisdom is the knowledge that there is no end to our negative characteristics if we submit to them. Greed is a perverted search for real security – security in God. We are caught in the materialistic trap because we have it in mind that this is where our security lies and, therefore, competitiveness is necessary. The result of it is that man is at war with everything around him. We are cutting each other's throats. Basically, the source of this energy drive is the same as *himmah*. It is *himmah* diverted towards purely materialistic gains. In the end, we cannot keep our goods in the house because of burglars, and so they all end up in a safe, which we do not have easy access to because it is in another city. Where does it end? It does not require a great deal of intelligence to reach the conclusion, if only we follow it through. But we are usually mediocre and apathetic. We keep on consuming and collecting and postpone facing our reality until it is too late.

If, however, we do not compromise and if we have a burning desire, if we face ourselves – then there is a chance. But we do not love ourselves enough, we do not respect ourselves enough, and therefore we cannot really love anybody else. If you love yourself totally and truly, then you love everybody else; but in this society the word 'love' is abused, misused, and its reality is not known to most of us.

Awareness and being

The extent of our awareness and discrimination are entirely the result of our inner energy and inner reality. Awareness comes if we take stock of ourselves – and not just for two minutes before we sleep, or once a week in a church or a mosque. If, without judgement – because judgement fragments awareness and creates a split – we become aware, we experience the thrill of pure awareness. Awareness is spontaneous and immediate. If you are totally aware, then your energy, your mind, is not dissipated by recalling anything from the past. That means that the memory bank is at its maximum efficiency, and that your energy is totally preserved and available now. We have a certain amount of energy at any given time. If you preserve that energy, you will experience the thrill of beingness – even if the experience is basically unwelcome, such as pain. If you can just be aware of the pain, you will have an amazing experience.

What we are talking about is very subtle. Your body must be at its best state; you cannot talk to people who are in physical pain and whose minds are agitated. You must be in a quiet place, in a reasonable environment, otherwise you cannot begin to exercise awareness. So catch yourself whenever you can, without judgement. Experience the beauty and the joy of beingness. Catch yourself when you are angry, and you will see that you are anger itself. Catch yourself at a moment of fear, and you will find you have become fear, and that in reality there is no fear. Who is afraid of whom? You will find that it is all your own doing. All these things are the projection of the mind due to the 'I'. I am afraid that an event which took place in the past may repeat itself. I am afraid because it hurt me then.

Fear and freedom

Fear is one of the biggest curses we inflict upon ourselves. If you face your self, you will find that it does not exist. The secret is to catch yourself the moment it occurs.

We all want freedom – inner freedom. We want freedom from our own imposition upon ourselves. We want freedom from the thorns of our self, by opening, expanding, and submitting to God. Outwardly, we must be disciplined. We must begin from the grossest – we can only begin from the outside. Animals eat, sleep, and reproduce, and die without worry. We do the same things and die full of worry, and yet call ourselves higher beings! And we create much more havoc and harm than animals. When animals have had enough food, they leave; but not man, for he continues to take revenge. Why? Because he has left the worship of God, and is worshipping the self.

Quietening the mind

We are all worshippers. But we must be cognizant of what we are worshipping. Islam is the essence of surrender and correct orientation and giving up the 'I'. We are all trying to reduce the pain caused by the mind. The man behind the conveyor belt in a hot assembly plant consoles himself with a plan for two weeks' holiday. What happens during those two weeks' holiday? He does not want to be disturbed. He wants to quieten his mind. The urge to quieten the mind is in everyone of us. The difficulty is in finding a method of doing it, so that we can put the pieces of the shattered self together.

So awareness and discrimination are basically our real human characteristics. As we become more aware, we become more discriminating. We know what is good or bad. We also know that private acts are often essentially harmful to ourselves. That is why we carry them out in darkness. When we do a good act, we tend to advertise it. We know and want to encourage that which is good and avoid the bad. Next we have to recognize the motive for our actions. However, we must not dwell on it much. We have to replace our so-called bad acts with good acts, in order to move on, in order to finish off the 'I', which is the source of all problems. There is no other problem. 'I' am the only problem. I am in my own way. There is nothing else. How to do away with me is a displacement process, an elimination process by God. The more you disappear, the more God appears.

The Prophet said, 'You are closest to Allah in prostration.' The act of prostration, in our prayers, is when you are in the lowest position, when your head is on the ground. That is the only position when the heart is placed higher than the head. The heart is the connecting vehicle, the vehicle through which we throb. When the heart and the head are united, then, and only then, are our actions correct and we are human beings. In prostration the heart is overlooking, overseeing, and there is the least of you because you have the least profile – there is less of the visible profile, and more of the inner profile.

The less there is in the outward, the more there is in the inward. The secret of one is the other. The source of one is in the other. The secret of the night is in the day. From maximum darkness comes greatest light. So the less there is of 'I', cause of pain and hankering, the more there is of self-fulfilment. The more there is discrimination, the more there is self-fulfilment, the more there is correctness, the more there is balance and spontaneity. Discrimination is our real nature. The more you are aware, the more you will be discriminating, the more you will be acting spontaneously and not reacting, and thereby be alive and joyful.

Surrendering oneself

The more you surrender yourself, the closer you are to God. The more I suffer, the less my mind meets its expectations, and the more I try to numb it or close in on it. Numbing is a perverted form of surrender. We are all trying to give up the mind and surrender one way or another. Surrender into the highest and you will reach the highest. The Prophet Jesus called those with heavy burdens upon their shoulders to come and throw the weight on him and be relieved. Jesus was not talking to a railway porter with baggage. He was calling anyone with burdens and heaviness of mind to surrender that which was their own making.

Unless there is real surrender of the 'I' there can be no freedom. Like all other laws, this is another true law, a very subtle law. We give up the 'I' by recognizing its dependent existence, its falsehood. It disappears like a fever. To reach that, we need discipline and help. Even the material responsibility towards a family is a help. If, at the moment, I am full of myself, my vanity and my arrogance, then if I have a spouse and innocent children and other dependants, maybe my heart will soften and I will begin to share with others and reduce my self-centredness. Expansion occurs by giving up a little, even if the reason is a child.

Although the beginning of surrender is hard, when expansion sets in, the self diminishes and bursts, like a bubble, as though it had never existed. For in reality there is only God; we are from God, and to God we return. All is totally dependent. There is nothing other than that reality. Everything else is superimposed upon it. The body is a physical growth superimposed upon the soul. The purpose of existence is to use the body for this discovery and to reach reality, and if we have not attempted that yet, we have simply abused a lot of oxygen and a lot of food. So the urgency is dependent on the extent of energy we can conserve, preserve and channel correctly towards the goal. No freedom can come unless we travel the path of self-unfoldment with clear boundaries and self-discipline.

A drop in the ocean contains the characteristics of the entire ocean, if only we are subtle enough to discern its secret. The secret of the ocean is in every drop. The secret of reality, the Secret-Giver, is in every heart. Life in one man is not superior or inferior to life in another. Life is from God and it is through a purified heart that we begin to see the beauty and the glory and the scintillating moment, the now-ness, the fullness of now. The intoxication of life, pure living. The totality and integrity of it all.

Microcosm and macrocosm

Man is the microcosm, and the outside world is the macrocosm. At the moment, we are not synchronized or aligned. The microcosm 'I' is not tuned to the macrocosmic world, therefore I suffer due to lack of understanding and am under the heavy weight of the ignorance which would lift once the tuning of the microcosm to the macrocosm occurs. This occurs through surrender, through giving up the 'I' which is the cause of the misalignment. Its elimination will illumine the alignment of the microcosm with the macrocosm.

We are inseparable from the entire cosmos, for we are its reflection. The fact you can see a star means that the seed of consciousness of the star is in you. The fact that you understand generosity means that the consciousness of generosity is in you. You contain all in a miniature fashion. You cannot see it because you have said, 'I am this and that', and have thereby superimposed the illusions of the self.

We have said that the beginning of surrender is hard, but when one begins to give up the self begins to diminish. Giving up materially is the start. Then one has to give up inwardly, which is what we are talking about: giving up the 'I'. God will make the path easy for whoever fears God. But those who fear other than God are at a loss.

> And as for him who is mean
> and thinks himself independent
> of the needs and desires of the best path,
> We will ease for him the path to affliction
> and his wealth will not avail him when he perishes.

The two directions are clearly described. The security of wealth is of no avail when the end is near, so why can't one remember that now?

As we invest, we reap. The less we have physically or of the self, the lighter and freer we are. The meaner one is, the poorer one is at the end. For everything we do, we are awarded accordingly and instantaneously. We put our parents in old people's homes and we too end up the same way. In the East, we used to have life and death next to each other in the same household. Children were born in the same household harbouring old people. There were few privacies and separations. But now we too in the East are living in two-bedroom apartments, facing television and eating frozen dinners and quarrelling.

Allah says

On Us the guidance

It is upon Us to show you the Path. Guidance is in our heart. We are following the inner guide when we truly submit to Allah.

And Ours is the Hereafter and the beginning

If we pay attention to the 'afterlife', we gain this life and the afterlife. If we pay attention only to this life, we will lose both. Action and result are not separate. The result of action is according to the intention. If my intention is good, so will the result be.

So I warned you of the fire that flames.

If we are not in the coolness of real contentment and on the path of ease, we are bound for the agitation of the Fire. We know the meaning of fire inside. We know what it is when we are burning with fear, anger or disappointment. No one reaches the Fire except the fool who does not heed the warning.

The Path is clear, in black and white. Allah says,

> None shall be cast in the Fire but the wretched,
> He who denied and turned his back.

So this is the warning, that if we do such and such, the result will be such and such. If we do not pay attention to the law of gravity, we will fall and break our neck. It is pure logic, action and reaction. If we have attachment, we will suffer as a result.

If you worship other-than-God, you will pay the price for it.

> And will avoid the Fire
> he who fears Allah (who guards against evil).
> He who gives his wealth to purify himself.

Our fears are of other-than-God when we are pursuing our self.

Giving is the start of expansion and freedom from attachment and enslavement. Giving is the purifier of wealth and the giver. In Islam we have to give a certain amount of our wealth each year. By purification, there also comes improvement and increase. Outwardly, we pay a tax; inwardly it is cleansing. The more we give, the more it becomes. And we find those who are completely generous – it is as though they had access to unlimited wealth. The person who fears God, the person who pays his tax, purifies his wealth, not because of the internal revenue service, but because he comprehends the wisdom of the tax and lives its reality.

> And he does this without expectation
> of favour or recompense. Save seeking
> the pleasure – the Face of his Lord, the High,
> And soon he shall be content and satisfied.

So the Path is clearly indicated in the Qur'an and through the indications one reaches certainty. One vital aid on the Path is the keeping company of other seekers of God. The world we are living in now is so tumultuous, uncertain, and treacherous, that no matter what security we try to hang onto, we shall find it shaky, materially and otherwise. The importance of right companionship is more vital now than at any other time. Trust among ourselves can only be enhanced if we have the right company, because we basically want to trust. A lot of energy is dissipated when we are distrustful.

11

Unity

There is only Unity. Everything has come from God and
returns to Him, and everything other-than-that is an illusion.
Having said that, having grasped it intellectually, we have
to experience it. There is nothing else to do. Man has been
created in order to see and experience the illusion he has
inflicted upon himself. This is the reason why Muhammad
came. He did not bring anything new. He simply purified
and updated what had come before him many, many times.
Even most of the rituals and the code of behaviour were
already there. The divinely revealed way of life had degener-
ated, it had been perverted and diluted. All that the Prophet
did was to redefine it, and confine it – and also to make it
sweet. Circumstances had changed and the style of living,
the way of development of mankind had reached a point
whereby Allah, through the Qur'an and his last Messenger,
gave us the ultimate code of conduct.

Nothing in this life can mean anything unless it is contained. Nothing whatsoever can be looked at, defined, ex-
changed, or understood – unless it has a boundary. *Sharī'ah*
the revealed law of Islam, is the boundary, or the code of
conduct and behaviour of human beings. Every path has its
own code of conduct, be it wide or narrow, zigzagged or
straight. A path is defined by its boundaries.

At the moment, for most of us, unity is an act of faith, until
such time as we experience it in everything we look at, and
do not see duality or separation. One sees everything as it
is, then, in its reality, without confusion. This is what every
human aspires to know and experience. By not knowing, we
are in confusion and we are agitated by our ignorance. We are

agitated because it is in our nature to want to know, and it is in our nature to want to see the unity in everything. If we put aside our personal value judgements, likes and dislikes, wants and rejections, happiness or unhappiness with each particular situation, then, with reflection and contemplation, we would begin to see how everything is related to everything else in the broad network of unity.

This is the beginning of seeing the unifying factor in this life and beyond. It is not a romantic notion when the muslim says there is no god-other-than God. It is not fantasy or negative attitude when we say we belong to God and to Him we return. This means that there is nothing other-than-that from which we came and to which we return. And so we understand and accept the situation, not fatalistically and negatively, but with knowledge and therefore contentment. Unity is seeing this, in order to establish and understand the chain of cause and effect. The science of unity is the science of self-knowledge. Islam is about this – about the worshipping of God, Who is the source of everything, from Whom everything has come and unto Whom everything returns and in Whom everything is unified.

Integration and interrelatedness

We are at the moment looking at small systems in this globe or in this cosmos. The greater the aspiration of the scientist, the more you find he wants to take the knowledge of that system to its boundary – in order to see that everything else is linked up with it, in order to interrelate. This is why in our universities nowadays you can find a multi-disciplinary approach to almost any topic. All aspects are examined in order to relate them to each other. Nothing is in isolation – no system, no atom, no insect, no wavelength or vibration. Everything affects what is around it and vice versa. The difficulty is that we cannot measure these influences. Indeed, the extent of cause and effect is often so subtle that we cannot measure or recognize it. A tiny sparrow that has dived into a wood affects the ecology of the wood – to a very small extent, it is true, but the effect is there.

Everything interacts in this world. Everything is related through a web. Looking at it from a subtler point of view, how did anything arise in this world, how did anything come to be? Every event must have a cause, whether we recognize the cause or not. When we do not recognize the chain, it is only due to our ignorance. Every event has a cause, every son has a father. And every effect, in turn, becomes the cause of something else. So it is a perpetual chain, the whole thing is one integrated model – unified. You cannot chop it up for the sake of convenience. You cannot say, 'This is my world and I have nothing to do with anything else.' Nevertheless, we constantly seem to try this impossibility on an individual or community or national basis. From this point of view, no country in the world is totally independent. We are all interdependent.

Man is greedy by nature; there is an echo in him wanting everything, because his essence is from That Which created everything – from God. So there is an echo in him that makes him want to reach God, but usually in a perverted way that seems the easy way. If we look at the ninety-nine Beautiful Names of God, which are the attributes of Allah, we find ourselves aspiring towards each one because, in reality, we are all aspiring towards God. We are all veering to reach that which is the Cause of everything, which is the Source of unity.

Islam as the Path to unity

Islam makes it very easy and the Path to this understanding and experience easy and swift, because Islam is clean, unedited, unabridged, and confirmed by many followers directly. We all know and accept the same identical Qur'an. We also know how the Prophet and his companions and his descendants behaved and conducted themselves in day-to-day situations. Some doctrines and religions have attempted to make their priesthood class or men of knowledge into intermediaries. Unfortunately, muslims in some countries have also fallen into this trap, into the trap of having middle men.

The Prophet traded, transacted, borrowed and loaned, lived in houses, had a family, and the smile never left his face. He did his best under all circumstances and was seen to act correctly and courageously. Whenever people started showing unnecessarily high regard or reverence for him, he reminded them that he was only the son of a woman, and that he was an orphan and a mortal like others. The Prophet was an example of humility and humanity, and to understand and imitate his behaviour is simple and accessible to all of us, if we want to. On the other hand, if we take things out of context, to suit ourselves and justify our actions, that too is very easy. We can pick out the tradition that suits us at the time and use it to fit or misfit our purpose! We only cheat ourselves.

We must scan the whole horizon. We cannot just take a bit of it and shut out the rest. We cannot be shut out from this world. We are subject to everything, in good health, bad health, poverty, wealth, friendship, enmity, everything. We are an integral part of it all. Inner understanding is already there, but we have covered our understanding by our illusion, by our fantasy, which is due to our own past habits and future expectations and fears, our so-called personality.

If is difficult to reach a point of full understanding of the basis, or building-block, or foundation of humanity which is totality-within-oneself, unless we go through a process that quickens this search by stripping step by step. This is surrender or elimination. So through Islam, through surrender, through giving-up, through prayer, through constant invocation of God, through turning back to God and, in order to be refreshed, in order to have our energies available to us, we begin to make progress.

Everyone wants self-fulfilment, and this state cannot come about without knowledge of the self, for the good and the bad seem to stem from the self. There is nothing other-than-God, Who has created the self. This is the message that the

Prophet Muhammad brought. So we begin by surrendering, depending only on God, and following the right code of conduct.

Islam is the path of ease, ease in the sense of knowing how to behave. How do we know how to behave? Call upon your heart, and take counsel with somebody near you, ask for help. Say 'I am disturbed – I do not know how to behave in these circumstances. Can you advise me?' Trust is the main thing, the base of Islam. If there is no trust, there is nothing.

As we have said, the first step is non-hypocrisy. Again, some of us take things too literally. Stopping hypocrisy does not mean terrorizing the world and saying how awful this and that is. You have not created the world. You do not know what the world is about. So the best thing one can do for oneself is to shut up to begin with. If I do not like this house, I don't have to make a fuss or lie about it. It does not do anybody any good. This is why the Prophet advised people not to say anything unless it is in its place, i.e. will serve a positive purpose towards the good.

Towards the good

Islam involves submitting to *sharī'ah*, to the code of correct conduct. And *sharī'ah* is a wide avenue, not a narrow alley. It is sweet, and it makes almost everything accessible and possible to man. It does not deny man in this world anything that is good for him. The restrictions of the code of conduct are to protect him from what harms him. If you look at these restrictions, in most instances what it does is to undermine hypocrisy and secretiveness, or not facing situations as they really are. The code of conduct always wants to reveal things. What the so-called advanced countries of the West are suffering from in the very individuality and privacy they have inflicted upon themselves. If our actions are good and selfless, we are not ashamed of them and do not hide them in dim rooms and behind curtains. Our selfish and vulgar acts usually are hidden from others. So there is a built-in behaviour pattern in us all, pointing towards the good.

The illusion is that the individual ends where his skin ends. This is the fallacy that we have inflicted upon ourselves. That is why we have all ended up in individual isolation. This is mine, my little house, my child, my religion, my nationality, etc. Our leading powerful nations consist of people huddling in their individual small houses or apartments, watching a dead cube, the television flickering away, a mirage. If this is what humanity or civilization is about, I pray for liberation from it.

What can the Western culture give us in terms of humanity? There are not many full human beings left. Most of us are dashing about on four wheels. I hardly see anybody using their legs. We are enslaved by material advancement in this culture, and this is what is preventing us from liberating ourselves from our illusion, from what we have inflicted upon ourselves in terms of expectations and desires, our past habits and norms. It is not liberating. It is imprisoning us further. If only we used our material progress properly, if only we knew when to say no.

We call ourselves a scientific society. How can a system grow indefinitely? Scientifically, every system has a boundary. The world places a limit on whatever it is. Maybe we have not at this moment reached the limit of our petroleum reserves, but every system inherently must have a limit, and everything has an end.

We were born on one day, only to die on another. Every day we are taking a step closer towards death. How many of us remember that? We all live as though we go on forever. The body will eventually go back to where it came from, because it is a bundle of minerals, borrowed for a few years from the earth, indirectly through food, and it must go back.

So who are we? We are not what we think we are. We have identified ourselves with this so-called individual being, the ego, the self brought about by mind and intellect. Mind is based on memory of the past which one wants to reproduce and perpetuate. At all times when we are acting in this world, we are trying to reproduce those things in our past that we liked and avoid those things that we did not like. This is what has enslaved us.

This, however, is not the whole story of humanity. Man is the most glorious being. He is the representative of God. And the choice is up to man to rise to his reality. The choice is up to him to give up that which is not real, which only exists as an echo, or as an image, or a shadow. This body exists because of life, and life is light, and light exists after death and was there before birth. It is my doing that I have identified with the self that causes me to suffer whenever there is an imbalance between my expectations, desires, and reality. It is my own doing. Islam brings about this realization quickly, and not only intellectually. It embraces it instantly. Remember that there is no god other than God and be grateful.

When you are grateful and content, you preserve your energies. If you are grateful for what you are now, at all times, then the system is in balance. Man is at all times in dynamic flux. From health, one goes to sickness, from day to night, from bad to good, from poverty to wealth. Everything is in motion one way or the other. So at any point you find that there are aspects that are acccording to your expectations, some you like, some you dislike. I could look at the empty part of this glass and I could say, 'This glass is not full,' or I could look at the full part of it. It is up to me to be content or otherwise. So when we do the prayer *salāt* in Islam, and we say praise be to God, the Lord of the World, at the beginning one may not mean it fully. Later on it becomes a habit, and I am bound to look at the positive because I can see myself that I could be worse off, in any other situation. So I thank the Creator.

There must be a creator for any act, for any product. The muslim has no problem. He says, 'Look, we come from Allah and to Allah we will return, and let's get on with it.' And that is tremendous. Many of us, however, have grown up in this 'intellectual' society, and this is the biggest curse. The stupidest man in the world is the 'clever' man. The simple man, the straight and honest one, is the winner in the long run. The simpler the approach, the easier. The child has a simple approach. Look at his face, his smile – spontaneousness. By and large, man becomes a hypocrite because he tries to be clever. He uses his intellect in a manner that he is not supposed to.

If we do not act spontaneously, a lot of our energies are dissipated. There is a limited amount of energy in any of us at any given time, energy that God has given us through this life and for this particular circumstance. If part of that energy is preoccupied with the past, preserving one's image, and part of that energy is concerned with the future, there is little or no energy left for the moment, and thus one is bound to fail in whatever endeavour is being undertaken.

Islam is about correct living, is about being decent to oneself. If I am not kind to myself to begin with, how can I be kind to anyone else? It is not possible. Charity starts at home. The first home we know is the home of the soul, this body – oneself. So we start with it. Often we find this difficult because we have become so corrupt, so we start with the neighbour. The neighbours are very noisy. It is always easy to look elsewhere and to attack others and neglect oneself. If we concern ourselves totally with rehabilitating our shattered selves, then a start has been made. Proper concern for oneself means non-hypocrisy, balance in thought and action, good manners in all situations, goodwill, honest and pure intentions. The result is fearless, joyful living. This is Islam. Islam is about decent living, full living, is about humanity, is about man – his totality and unity.

Man preserves and commands all his energies if he gives up his ego. If we do not give it up, if we are in conflict and dissipated, we are like a cracked jar. We then blame our dissipated energy on luck, circumstances, on bad neighbours, or whatever. There is no end to it. From our point of view, the buck stops with everyone of us, at the individual. You are the start and the end of the road. Preserve your energies. If we care for ourselves in this manner, then we can care for others. If, however, we care for ourselves only in a selfish way, there is no end to it – caring for my body, limbs, hair, only to give up the body later on to the worms in the tomb. I am not recommending reduction in cleanliness, but we do over-pamper the body. As it is, two-thirds of our lifetime is spent on looking after our body. Make use of it. It is only an instrument, a launching pad. A launching pad has to be used, has to be burnt – otherwise it is wasted.

Islam is not just niceties – outer courtesy and inner hypocrisy! For those of us who have come to the Path with love of the Prophet, and his descendants, we can copy and follow them to make it easy. But it is not necessary for us to have a mud house, emulating the Prophet because he had a mud house. We can have a modern house. It is the attitude of the man towards the house that matters. Islam makes it easy, makes it instantaneous, five times a day, a reminder to the man: five times of cleansing, of surrendering, of humility, of thanksgiving. It is less likely that the arrogant man, at the end of his prayers, will immediately get up and continue the arrogance he had before the start of the prayers.

So Islam makes the first step easy. When the mind is set free from past shackles and man is liberated from fear of future uncertainties, he can then look at each situation with spontaneity, purity, and clarity. The spontaneity of a child and the clarity of a man of wisdom – clarity in the sense of seeing circumstances in their totality, untarnished by our own expectations and biases. When we are not ourselves involved or attached, we can see the situation more clearly. Our energies are not partially dissipated through fear.

The muslim fears nothing except Allah. And therefore, his energy is not dissipated by fear of other-than-Allah. He is not afraid of his image, his reputation, nor is he afraid of the future, because he is depending on Allah and doing his best in the meantime.

Imam Ali says, 'Work for this life as though you are going to live forever.' At the same time Imam Ali said, 'Work for the Next Life as though you will die tomorrow.' This means one's deeds and actions for the Next Life are to be done now, urgently, while one's actions for this life can be postponed. Imam Ali was speaking of the correct priority that one should take in one's life.

By correct living, the muslim will have the right people wishing to be with him, and when he dies, they will miss him, remember him well and with a sense of loss. There is no better way of living in this world. If there is, then the individual has to discover it. The author certainly knows no other way.

Like a physical law, this is an absolute law. And all that remains is for the individual to discover it within himself. It is not imposed from outside, not because a man from Arabia came and said to do it, and we just have to do it. Try and find out yourself. You will reach the same point. All that happened is that the exalted being, through whom the Qur'an came, said it clearly, in so many ways and lived it fully. The message of the Prophet continues. The Prophet crystallized it and gave it to us as a gift. So when man is in this situation, he can act courageously, because he is in no fear of other-than-Allah.

In any negotiation, any transaction, if you are not worried about the result or outcome, you can act with all your energies. You act courageously and surprise everybody, but you are simply doing your best. With this attitude, you are bound to succeed. This is the doctrine of success in this world. It is for here and now. It is not superstitious fantasy. It is for immediate implementation. The extent to which we take Islam fully, live Islam fully, is dependent on the extent of our yearning. Without yearning, nothing happens, it will only remain as intellectual table talk. We can live the moment fully, while bound to the true Path. We have to contain ourselves, otherwise we will start a chain reaction that will completely throw us off.

Correct behaviour diffuses the dangers along the Path, diffuses all the harmful demands. Life is dynamic: at any moment, anything can happen. Clarification by the code of correct conduct diffuses the dangers and dispels the secrecy, privacy and all the hidden harms. That is why in Islam nobody spies on anybody else. When you enter a house, you must ask permission beforehand and greet the people as you enter. You do not enter by the windows or bug their telephones. Islam is the way human beings can live decently, behave well towards themselves and others, and thereby have the best possible time in this world. Islam is not about sitting around on thin cushions in dusty villages in Iran or Sudan and talking about the Garden, Hell, or life-after-death. It is a doctrine for the living. It has to be applied, seen as real by the individual. Otherwise, Islam will only remain in a book. What is the point, if the message of the Qur'an is not absorbed, lived, learned, and tested?

Allah says in the Qur'an, 'Make a contract with Me – loan Me.' Do something for God and see the results of it, because when you do something for God, it is not for other-than-God. It is not for reasons that are definable, which are, generally speaking, only going to reinforce the ego. The benefit is instantaneous.

Once we know how to conduct ourselves decently, we can act clearly and decisively. We can say what we mean. This is the basis of Islam. *'Īmān* (trust, belief, faith) comes along with that. Living Islam brings out the full human being and he will be a full believer *(mu'min)*, in the sense that we have come from Allah and we return to Allah, and this life is but a quick journey. We believe in everything that has been given to us, not just as a doctrine, or as a dead belief, but in order to actually be lived. If we act in total remembrance of God, we act as though God is watching our every step, everything that moves in our head, in our heart, until such time as we know.

These are all steps bordered by *sharī'ah*, by correct conduct. The beginning is a very wide avenue and it converges in the point of unity, in Allah.

So this is the ultimate end of the journey. The Path is easy and clear. The start may be difficult, but the end is easy. If we do our best all the time, trying to understand the source, trying to reach God, the more we expand the more we find there is no end to expansion. Everyone of us can and will expand, as it is the promise of God. How do we expand? By living it. When your energies are preserved, your abilities are sharpened, everything becomes clearer to you. There is no end to clarity, there is no end to this knowledge. And this knowledge comes in a different way – not through prescriptive or encyclopaedic means.

Our Prophet was not cluttered with prescriptive knowledge. You get the right knowledge at the time you need it, if your inner condition is right. According to our intentions, we will be rewarded. If my intention is good, correct, if it is not simply for additional material clutter and luxury, I am bound to reach the right knowledge.

If the intention is clear, even if the final result is not as expected, you are in the clear within yourself. It is the intention that determines the effect on you. Islam is the constant. Living Islam is the message, the technique of constantly purifying the most vital instrument, the heart: the instrument through which we know God, the instrument through which we know anything worthwhile. Anything of importance we know by our head or intellect. It is prescriptive, very easy: 'Do this, do that.' It is the higher knowledge that can only come through the purification of the heart, through the throbbing of a pure heart.

There is a reference in the Qur'an that says one must not touch the Qur'an unless one is clean. What this means is that one with an impure heart cannot even touch it, let alone understand it. It means we cannot even understand the outer meanings of it if our heart is not pure, because it is an immense book. It is the book of totality, the book of knowledge, and everything is in it.

To understand unity, we have first to rehabilitate ourselves, to integrate, unify and reconnect ourselves. We have to patch up this shattered being. Otherwise, we cannot talk about unity, or Islam. It will only remain an intellectual conversation, to no avail: barren , like most other pursuits.

We are interested in the science of beingness, to be, to live fully, as decent, responsible human beings – responsible in the full sense of the word. Allah says man was created as 'My *Khalīf* on earth'. *Khalīf* means representative. *Khalīf* means the man who has full power of attorney. Look how irresponsibly we act. We are destroying animals and the earth, What licence have we?

We are hanging on a breath. Our survival depends on a breath of air. Life is so delicate. Why do we not remember God?

Unless we take these steps, we are not qualified to discuss unity. We are not qualified to discuss the ultimate point of reaching the knowledge of reality. We cannot do it, unless we take the first step, then the second, and then the third. The first step is *dhikr* – remembrance at all times; the second is *fikr* – discrimination, which leads to proper behaviour; and the third is *himmah* – the drive towards the ultimate objective, self-knowledge, from which comes fulfilment.

Conclusion

Every conclusion has its root in its beginning; so to conclude this brief book we are reminded of the root of every motive that lies within each human being. At all levels of our growth and development we are driven by desire for good health, appropriate relationships, comfort, security, love. The beginning is therefore common to all of us. The child's horizons are limited, his expectations are small, and he operates within a very short time-scale. As the child grows the horizons widen, the depth of vision becomes more perceptive. Therefore, he encompasses a wider world but the same rules apply, in that the person wants to relate in a harmonious and balanced interactive fashion.

Life is a journey from dispersion and diversity to convergence and unity. We begin to perceive, through our outer senses, different signals and meanings which we try to relate to what we have already experienced in the past, and then build upon this past. This is how we widen the scope of the world of our comprehension. Our intellects grow as these experiences relate and multiply, while our outer reasoning expands as a result of our intellectual development.

Our inner integration and harmony develops with the growth of that phenomenon of insight or higher intellect that is often referred to as the awakening of the heart. As a person evolves and as his life unfolds we find greater interrelationship between the intellectual understanding, the causal understanding and the inner awareness and awakening. This phenomenon is what we are all after in our human journey. We all desire total, integrated self-unfoldment whereby the human being is the interspace between intellectual, mechanistic, logical understanding and an inner, purer, not so quantifiable awareness and awakening. Thus man is at all times leading towards this total interspace situation, part of him is intellect, part of him is the inner, unfathomable, indescribable reflector of another zone of consciousness – a person who will eventually reach the shores of an infinite Reality.

In the early stages we perceive physical and material realities and will pursue them. As we progress we touch on increasingly subtle realities, which all impinge, interact and interrelate with the outer realities. The separation between them is not discernible or measurable and the barrier between them is the interspace that constitutes the human being in his totality.

Man's need to make sense of his physical, material environment and the causal relationships of this world is a prelude and necessary condition for the development of the powers of reasoning and intellect which will ultimately lead him to the awakening of those higher faculties which lie dormant within him. It is as though man has grown from a mineral background into a plant background, from plant towards an animal form and eventually to a higher human state which reflects the story beyond.

In a great many mystical heritages and religions we find the analogy that man is a reflector of the cosmos and everything that is perceivable outside lies dormant within man, and that life on earth unfolds until that point when one perceives and hears completely the echo of total creation within oneself. This is the ultimate gift that will bring contentment and satisfaction to the heart of man. No material, physical or intellectual achievement will bring that self containment and self contentment with its true and voluntary submission to Reality in its totality.

We are all enslaved by our material and physical limitations, yet we detest limitations. This is the proof that ultimately within us lies a door that opens up onto a limitless horizon. The approach to this door is through increased limitation and abandonment. Man's innermost desires will guide him towards the Path that will save him from the terrors of darkness and ignorance. He desires tranquillity, contentment, love and harmony. He will learn to achieve these objectives first through outer physical limitations and ultimately inwardly, which goes beyond the physical and material barriers. Man is in this world but he does not belong to it. He has come here on a journey in order to discover his Source and his ultimate destiny.